# FIFTH SERIES
# Modern Collector's Dolls

Patricia R. Smith

Cover doll is 42″ "Daddy's Girl" by Ideal. Courtesy Kay Bransky.

**COLLECTOR BOOKS**
*A Division of Schroeder Publishing Co., Inc.*

The current values in this book should be used only as a guide. They are not intended to set prices, which vary from one section of the country to another. Auction prices as well as dealer prices vary greatly amd are affected by condition as well as demand. Neither the Author nor the Publisher assumes responsibility for any losses that might be incurred as a result of consulting this guide.

Cover doll is 42" "Daddy's Girl" by Ideal. Courtesy Kay Bransky.

Printed by IMAGE GRAPHICS, INC., Paducah, Kentucky

# DEDICATION

Volume V of the Modern Collector's Dolls Series is dedicated to all friends across the United States, Canada, England, Australia, France, Germany and the Netherlands. Friendships are more important than any thing else in our world of doll collecting.

# CREDITS

All photographs are by Dwight F. Smith unless noted following name of owner.
Hazel Adams, Jayn Allen, Ruth Anderson, Carolyn Altfather (Margaret Mandel), Austin Collection, Lilah Beck, Sally Bethscheider, Jackie Barker, Elinore Bibby, Kay Bransky, Sylvia Bryant, Bessie Carson, Betty Casteel, Nancy Catlin, Doris Chandler, Bonnie Chichura, Donna Colopy, Betty Cossiboin, Rosalind Cranon, Linda Crowsey (Glen Ray), Renie Culp, Virginia Dean, Donnie Durant, Barbara Earnshaw, Marie Ernst, Edith Evans, Kathy Feagan, Joleen Flack, Michelle Freeman, Sally Freeman, Carol Friend, Eloise Godfrey, Karen Heidemann, Bernice Heister, Mimi Hiscox, Marilyn Hichcock, Diane Hoffman (Steve Schweitzberger), Phyllis Houston, Donna Hodge (Richard Hodge), Virginia Jones, Dorothy Judge, Kimport Dolls, Roberta Lago, Phyllis Lemanski, Mr. Beppe Garella-Lenci, Beres Lindus, Nancy Lucas (Sally Freeman), Wynonia Lurie, Margo Mandel, Margaret Mandel, Jeannie Mauldin, Marge Meisinger, Amy and Shirley Merrill (Brent Merrill), Mrs. Arthur Messer, Karen and Wendi Miller, Dorothy Mulholland, Louise Nixon, Judy Olive, Grace Otto, Anita Pacey, Ricky Paez, Shirley Pascuzzi (Mike Stehlin), Judy Perez, Penny Pendlebury (Chuck Pendlebury), Ruth Rivasi, Susan Rogers, Evelyn Samec, Sheryl Schmidt, Rosemary Schneider, June Schultz, Jeannie Shipi, Martha Silva, June Sloniger, Gertrude Smith, Jewel Smith, Robert Smith, Shirley Smith, Mary Stolzenberg, Martha Sweeney, Phyllis Teague, Lynette and Pat Timmons, Treasure Trove (19 Village Rd. Manhasset, NY), Majorie Uhl, Arlene Wacker, Peg Webster (Sally Freeman), Freda Webster (Brent Merrill), Ann Wencel, Chester Wencel, Mary Wheatley, Mary Williams, Betty Wood (Carol Friend), Glorya Woods, and Beatrice Wright.

# NEW AND ADDITIONAL INFORMATION FROM FIRST FOUR VOLUMES

The Advance Doll Company put out a Black walking doll called "Maybelle" which looked just like "Wanda The Walking Wonder."

Pat Sebastian sent the information that she received from the H.D. Lee Company concerning the Coca-Cola uniforms. The letter states that the tan uniform with green stripes was originally intended to be used outside by the drivers and the white with green stripes for use in the plants. However, the white was much more popular and in the warmer parts of the country, it was worn outside as well as inside. Also the composition "Buddy Lee" dolls were made until 1949 then changed to hard plastic which were produced until 1962 or 1963. In reference to the color of the Coca-Cola uniforms, we are sure this is just the explanation as to why two colors were made.

The Deluxe Toy Creations' "Sweet Rosemary" was designed by Sheukwan and on the market in 1957. They will be marked AE-25. "Sweet Rosemary" came in several different outfits: # 102, ruffled blue party gown of net with silver metallic threads and bows; #103, pink layered lace with velvet sash and pink lace gloves; #104, blue net gown with "mink" stole, has long sleeves; #–105, nurse uniform and blue/red cape; #106, red short dress with white yoke and bolero jacket.

Mary Griffith sent the information that the doll shown on page 200 of *Modern Collector's Dolls, Vol. 3* has a red felt hat with elastic under the chin and a tag: ALL NEW MATERIALS/CONTENTS/POLY 100%/HORSMAN DOLLS INC./P.O. BOX 1390/COLUMBIA, S.C. 29202/REG. NO. PA. 114 MASS. T-21.

Lelani Blessing sent the following regarding the 8" Jockey and Hunter listed in *Modern Collector's Dolls, Vol. 1* on page 231 under Mfg. Unknown. These dolls were first produced by Pressman Toy Corp. in 1963, and the first year they were on the market there were three dolls: "Jockey," "Fox Hunter" and "Western Rider." There were also horses and extra accessories. The second Year (1964) they added a girl Fox Hunter.

Anne Dozier sent us the correct date that the puppet "Teto" by Hazelle on page 247 *Modern Collector's Dolls, Vol. I.* It was 1961, not 1952.

Bessie Carson shares this information on the Nancy Ann Storybook cabinet. The cabinet is 25" wide, 44" tall and 5¾" deep. It is off-white lined with pale blue and it is made of wood with fiber board back. The label on the back is 3½" x 2½" and reads: STORYBOOK DOLL CABINET/MANUFACTURED EXCLUSIVELY FOR/NANCY ANN DRESSED DOLLS/INSTRUCTIONS/IF GLASS FRONT IS DESIRED, ORDER/FROM YOUR LOCAL GLASS GLAZIER FOR/EACH SHELF. SIZE 7 11/16" X 24 1/8"/SINGLE STRENGTH WITH ROUNDED CORNERS AND POLISHED EDGES. There is a slot down the full height of the cabinet on each side for sliding the glass in and out, and a slot at the bottom and top of each shelf for holding the glass.

Betty Tait adds this information on the "Queen Elizabeth" 11" doll in *Modern Collector's Dolls Vol I*, page 117. She has the same doll and it has an original Peggy Nesbit tag. Her doll bears a black tag (present ones are red) that states: QUEEN ELIZABETH II IN STATE ROBES.

If you should happen onto an all-cloth doll with a doorman's uniform, with a doorman's cap reading "Henri Bendel," it is a "Buster Doll," made after, and named for, the real doorman at Henri Bendel's, a Manhattan, New York, department store. "Buster" is the nickname of James Jarret, Jr. who was 86 and still working in 1980 when the doll was made. He had worked at Henri Bendel's for 70 years and was given the name "Buster" by the founder due to his young age when he started working there. The doll was made by a small craft group in Tennessee and sold for $15.00 at the Henri Bendel store.

The "Granny" doll shown on page 115 of *Modern Collector Dolls, Vol. III* is "Ma Brown," an advertising doll for Ma Brown Pickles. She had wire glasses and an apron with name printed on it.

# CONTENTS

15″ "Norwegian." All composition with mohair wig and sleep blue eyes. Closed mouth, separate thumbs and all fingers of both hands molded together and slightly curled. Tag: /STYLE LEADERS/FIFTH AVENUE DOLLS/MFRS. ADRENA DOLL CO. NEW YORK/. Back of tag stamped: NORWEGIAN. Doll is unmarked. (Courtesy Sally Freeman)

9″ "Ma-Lou." All deep brown sateen cloth with oil painted features and dressed in original red/white check gown with red head bandana and stole. This doll also came in a 15″ size with felt features. The apron is white. Tag is a photograph of a lady cooking pancakes with printing: "MA-LOU"/THE GREEN ORCHID. On reverse side: THIS IS A /LEDA H. PLAUCHE/PRODUCT/PAT. DESIGN 97,092. Purchased about 1938. (Courtesy Gertrude Smith)

13½″ "Campbell Kid" designed by Grace Drayton. This artist also was well known for her magazine drawings of "Dolly Dingle," and the two as dolls resemble each other very much. Cloth body with composition head and limbs. Straight legs and both hands have 2nd and 3rd fingers molded together. Molded yellow painted hair with deep side part and locks on the forehead. Painted features. Marks: E.I.H. CO. INC. Made by Horsman Doll Co. ca. 1925. (Courtesy Virginia Jones)

16″ "Buttons," the advertising doll for Dan River sheets and made by Inez Holland House. This ad is from the December issue of *American Home Magazine* of 1947. She has black yarn braids, large black button eyes, blue button nose on a mask face of fabric. The dolls do not have the cross stitches shown in the center seam. All cloth, flesh colored body and limbs. Came in a checkered dress, as well as a striped dress.

18″ "Country Girl" available from the Green Giant Co. with $2.50 and 2 labels from Green Giant Peas. 1956. Vinyl head with rooted hair, latex one piece body and limbs. The dress is white with green dots and removable white apron with company emblem printed on it. White hat with green trim. The 1957 dress was green/white check blouse with yellow buttons, yellow pinafore dress with green trim, white shoes & socks and yellow bonnet, plus carried yellow shoulder bag with check strap.

11″ Cut and sew "Merry," "Minx" and "Mike" offered at 25¢ per doll in 1953 and will be marked GENERAL FOODS 1953. Offered by Birds Eye Concentrated Orange Juice. "Merry" is a girl and has braids wich were attached by a separate piece of cloth on which they were printed. Ads were in *Family Circle Magazine*, as well as *Ladies Home Journal* and others.

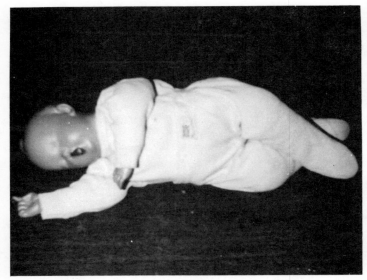

21″ "Hanes Baby" with cloth body, vinyl head and limbs. The hair is molded and the eyes are molded closed with painted lashes, open/closed yawning mouth and tongue. Wears two piece sleepers with the Hanes tag on front. The outfit came in mint green, blue and pink. Made in 1951 and marked: HORSMAN, although many are unmarked. (Courtesy Jeannie Mauldin)

13″ "Poppin Fresh" all one-piece cloth with glued on blue eyes. Pull string talker. Tag: MATTEL/POPPIN FRESH DOUGHBOY/PILLSBURY. 1969 Mattel, Inc. (Courtesy Jeannie Mauldin)

14″ Pillsbury Doughboy, "Poppin Fresh." All one piece stuffed cloth with printed on blue tie, blue eyes. POPPIN FRESH, on hat. 1971. (Courtesy Jeannie Mauldin)

4″ to 6″ "Pogo and Friends" advertising dolls. All vinyl, jointed only at the neck. Made for Proctor & Gamble. "Albert Alligator" marked: 1969 WALT KELLY, on bottom of foot; "Churchy La Femme" marked 1969 on foot; "Pogo Possum" marked 1969 WALT KELLY on foot; "Beauregard Hound": 1969 WALT KELLY, on foot; "Howland Owl": 1969 WALT KELLY, on foot. Not pictured is: "Porky Porcupine." All made in Japan. Found in such products as: Biz, Spic & Span, Oxydol, Tide, and Cascade. The year they were offered is the same year that comic strip creator, Walt Kelly, died. 1975. (Courtesy Jeannie Mauldin)

13½″ All one piece printed cloth chicken. Red comb and feathers with yellow bill and feet. Marks: CHICK-FIL-A, on front and DOODLES, on back. ca. 1970's. (Courtesy Jeannie Mauldin)

19″ "Mr. Peanut." Left doll has shorter feet than right doll, plus is printed same on back as on the front. Both are printed, stuffed cloth. 1970's. (Courtesy Jeannie Mauldin)

19″ "Elsie the Cow." All stuffed cloth with vinyl head. Original clothes. Made for Borden Milk Co. 1977. (Courtesy Martha Sweeney)

9½″ "Jolly Green Giant." All vinyl that is made in two pieces and fits together at the hips. His construction is very much like an old fashioned candy container. Marks on box: PRODUCT/PEOPLE/INC./TRADE-MARK OF THE GREEN GIANT/COMPANY AND USED WITH THEIR PERMISSION. 1970's.

*The Oakland Tribune* of Monday, May 12, 1980, ran an item by United Press International: "LOS ANGELES-Take 302 pounds of pastry dough, fill it with 50,000 strawberries, cover with 350 gallons of strawberry glaze and 300 cans of whipped topping. It makes a fine candidate for the world's largest strawberry pie. But that's not all. It will take about 300 man hours of labor to do it all, and then a 35 foot tractor-trailer rig is needed to haul it. It will measure 17 feet by 24 feet and weigh just over two tons.

Next, hand out 6,000 paper plates, 9,000 napkins and 6,000 forks. Bob's Big Boy Restaurant is making the pie to benfit the American Heart Association and television actor Vic Tayback, "Mel" of the T.V. series "Alice" will cut the first piece. The May 22 event in Century City is expected to net about $5,000.00 for the Heart Association. The pie, incidentally, will have about 2.6 million calories!"

9″ All vinyl "Big Boy" with coin slot in back of head. Jointed at neck with one piece body and limbs. Painted features and clothes. Marks: A PRODUCT OF BIG BOY RESTAURANTS OF AMERICA. MARCOTT COPR. 1973 on right foot. (Courtesy Betty Wood)

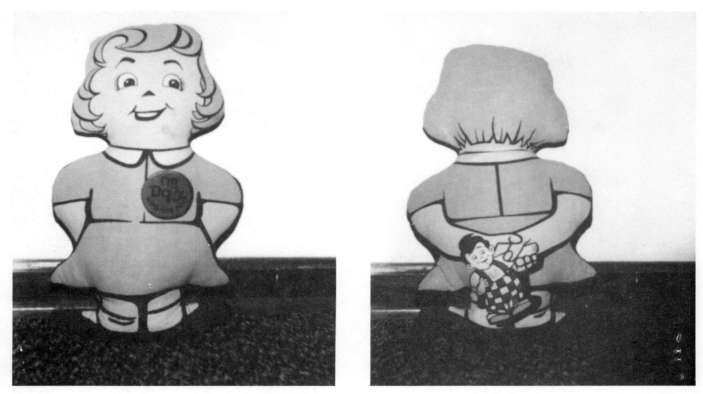

16″ "Dolly," Shoney's ad doll. All cloth with printing on clothes and features. The pin on front is also printed, and says: I'M DOLLY. WHO ARE YOU? Holds a "Big Boy" that is printed in the back. 1977. (Courtesy Jeannie Mauldin)

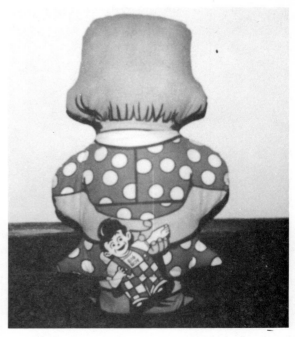

Front and back views of Dolly's polka dot dress that is all cloth, along with the all cloth "Big Boy." 1978. (Courtesy Jeannie Mauldin)

8″"Snap," "Crackle," and "Pop." All vinyl with molded on cloth. All are marked: T.M. OF THE KELLOGG CO. on bottom of feet. Box: PRODUCT PEOPLE/MINN., MINN. 1977. (Courtesy Jeannie Mauldin)

21″ "Ronald McDonald." Painted vinyl head, hands and shoes. Cloth body and limbs. Comes with whistle. Push stomach to blow whistle. Has purple "Grimace" in pocket. Marks: MCDONALD CORP., on head. Tag: 1978 MCDONALD CORP. HASBRO INDUSTRIES. (Courtesy Mary Wheatley)

19″ "Burger King." All stuffed cloth with painted vinyl head, crown and hands. Holds foam hamburger in one hand and has trick scarf in other hand. Secret pocket on side. Comes with childs ring (shown in belt) and instructions. Removable cape. Hair and crown are vinyl and part of the head. 1980.

6″ "Diaparene" Baby. Vinyl with molded, painted features. White diaper. Premium doll from Diaparene baby products. Marks: STERLING DRUG, INC. 1980. (Courtesy Mary Wheatley)

Line up of Gerber Babies. Front row, left to right: White version made by Uneeda Doll Co. 1972; very rare, first Gerber baby of 1936, 8″ and all cloth; Black version of the 1972 Uneeda doll; Lop-sided smile doll with small bib, 1966 version made by Arrow Industries. The last in bottom row is the 1955 doll made by the Sun Rubber Co. The two large dolls in the back row were made by the Atlanta Novelty firm, the Black in 1980 and the White from 1979 on.

Left is the 1981 limited edition bisque Gerber baby with a lot of eyelette lacing. The right one is the 1982 version bisque in pink organdy. The baby was sculptured by Neil Estern and made in porcelain by Stephanie Shader China Dolls. Each are signed and numbered.

The Gerber Baby is also available in a trunk with layette and is a drink-and-wet doll. Still has the cloth body, but has tube that runs through it. 1982. (Courtesy Phyllis Teague)

Close up of the nursing drink-and-wet Gerber Baby so the hole in the mouth can be seen. (Courtesy Phyllis Teague)

21″ "Mermaid" advertising doll for the Chicken of the Sea firm owned by Ralston Purina Company. She is vinyl with rooted blonde hair in long braids, sleep eyes and comes with her own tripod stand. The fish scales are red, has an adult figure and jointed waist. The red scales were made in 1965 and they were white in 1966. She comes with heart necklace and has earrings, as well as cloth around top as shown. Marks: MERMAID DOLL COMPANY 1965. (Courtesy Rosemary Schneider)

# MADAME ALEXANDER
## DOLLS

The oldest, and rarest of the Madame Alexander dolls will always be sought after, but 1983 was a "slowing down" period for buying the *new* dolls and in many parts of the country the store shelves will have Madame Alexander dolls on the shelves to sell once more. The reason for this is that the "secondary" market which grew to such proportions in 1981 and 1982 (when every doll was purchased immediately with most going to flea markets and doll shows at twice the store prices) has slowed significantly. This came about when the store owners became aware of the practice and started to increase their own prices to match those outside the retail circle. In fact, buying in both areas has slowed down. Many new collectors are turning to other doll companies as they feel "cheated" by all sellers involved, retail or secondary market. Also, a great many stores dropped their accounts as the "hassel" of handling Madame Alexander dolls became too much for what they got out of it! NEW AND REVISED INFORMATION: From the second set of "Presidents Ladies" it will be noted that Tyler came in both blue and pink gowns.

During Christmas of 1980 the F.A.O. Schwarz firm offered a 14" "Pussy Cat" baby in a trunk, with extra wardrobe. ONLY the outfit on the doll will be tagged *Madame Alexander*. The other clothes are: quilted bunting, dropseat pajamas, lace trimmed coat and bonnet and a flowered dress. The extra outfits are not tagged Alexander, as one is made in California, one made in the Philippines, and two from the Prestige Collection. This was the practice for these dolls sold in trunks over the years. Madame Alexander made only the original doll and other clothing was made for the company selling it in a trunk or wardrobe.

"Madeline-Madelaine" was named for the little French girl and her friends, characters in books written by Ludwig Bemelmus.

Boy made of chamois with oil painted features and a blonde caracul wig. Separate thumbs and all fingers stitched together as are the Lenci dolls. He is impressed on back of neck: MADAME ALEXANDER. Dressed in original two piece short pants and shirt with red and blue stripes, navy coat, and cap is missing. Side snap black shoes. (Courtesy Grace Otto)

Cloth "So-lite" style doll with pressed face mask and *flirty* (move side to side) *black pupiless eyes*, yellow yarn hair. Wrists and ankles are tied with ribbons. Tied to one arm is tag: TEENY TWINKLE/MADAME ALEXANDER. ALL RIGHTS RESERVED. PATENT PENDING. Tag shows the face of the doll. Other side of tag: THIS DOLL HAS BEEN NEVA-WET PROCESSED, WHICH RENDERS IT WATER REPELLANT. 1939. (Courtesy Grace Otto)

13" "Lively Cherub Baby." Felt face with dark pink felt eyes, yellow yarn lashes, and yellow yarn hair. Dressed in pale blue organdy gown with embossed white flowers, pink rayon jacket and matching bonnet. Has music box in body with wind key in back. Plays lullaby. Tag: MADAME ALEXANDER and part of tag is gone. 1939.

17″ "Dottie Dumbunnie," the fiancee to "Sir Lapin O'Hare." White muslin body with black flannel feet. White velvet head with yellow inside ears. Black buttons for eyes. White buckram hat with pink ribbons, pink gown with gloves and flowers attached at waist. Tag on back: MADAME ALEXANDER/NEW YORK. 1938. (Courtesy Bonnie Chichura)

A profile view of the "Dottie Dumbunnie" of 1938. (Courtesy Bonnie Chichura)

15″ (18″ to tip of ears). "Posey Pet," and so tagged. Plaid satin body and limbs, plush paws and head. Brown velvet sewn on feet and pink cotton sheen lined ears. Felt eyes, nose and mouth, (whiskers missing). Pinafore dress matches the body and the Madame Alexander tag is on the pinafore. Booklet is called *The Story of Bunny Esmond*, which was put out by The Esmond Mills, Inc. Esmond, Rhode Island (in 1944). Esmond Mills made blankets and the story is about a bunny tricked by a red fox and how he found that an Esmond blanket was as warm as his own coat of fur. Also offered in booklet was a photo of baby and bunny, a miniature Bunny Esmond Doll blanket and two games.

20″-21″ "American Tot" in original light blue self color coin dot taffeta dress with matching bonnet. Hem of dress edged in rose color taffeta. Bonnet has wide rose color taffeta ribbon ties and multi-color flowers. Flowers also on dress bodice. White imitation leather shoes with rayon socks. Shoes have side snaps. White organdy one piece teddy and half slip, (no lace on undies). Cotton tag on dress with red print: MADAME ALEXANDER/NEW YORK. 1937. Shown with 7½″ all original Lenci. (Courtesy Glorya Woods)

13″ child with blue and white checkered oil cloth body and limbs, with ivory color feet (may have been white). Oil painted face mask with large brown eyes. Yellow yarn hair, dressed in white pinafore with blue trim and matching bonnet. Tag: MADAME ALEXANDER/NEW YORK U.S.A. ca. 1940's. (Courtesy Mimi Hiscox)

25″ "Pitty Pat." Cloth clown with face mask and painted features. The outfit is tagged: PITTY PAT/MADAME ALEXANDER N Y U.S.A./ALL RIGHTS RESERVED. The outfit is in blues and red on white with red trim. Hat has been added. ca. 1949-1950. (Courtesy Mimi Hiscox)

White wicker basket of 1936 holds a set of 7½″ molded hair "Dionne Quints" in pastel blue, pink, green, yellow and lavender dresses. (Courtesy Jeannie Mauldin)

13″ "Betty." All composition with blue tin sleep eyes, blonde mohair wig and dressed in original blue and white striped dress. Right arm is bent at the elbow. Organdy collar and organdy ruffle inside matching bonnet. Replaced shoes and socks. 1935. (Courtesy Shirley Merrill)

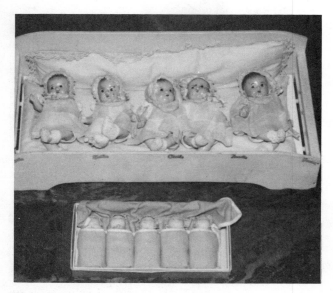

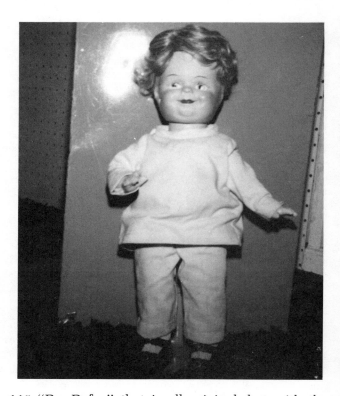

7½″ "Dionne Quints" of 1936-1937 shown in their wooden bed with their names on the side. The names are decals and there originally were three decals of flowers, one on each side and one in the middle. The box in front of bed shows a set of quints in blue bunting blanket with five "soap" dolls. (Courtesy Mary Williams)

14″ "Dr. Dafoe" that is all original, but with the stethoscope missing. All composition, character face with painted eyes. Original side part grey wig. Has right arm bent at elbow. Store tag: POQUE'S $1.95. 1936. (Courtesy Mary Stolzenberg)

Set of 8″ Dionne Quint toddlers in original pastel color romper suits, on pink satin pillow and in original wicker basket. Has other clothes attached to lid of basket. 1935-1936. (Author)

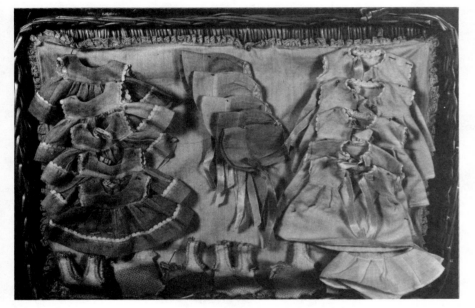

Shows extra clothing for the Dionne Quints that includes dresses, bonnets, slips and original swimsuits. All are in various shades of pastel colors. The original wicker basket has two handles and a rod that goes between two loops on front. (Author)

Set of Dionne Quints that are the 7½″ bent-leg babies of 1935-1936, showing their original white wooden crib, playpen, tricycle, potty chair and high chair. (Courtesy Shirley Smith)

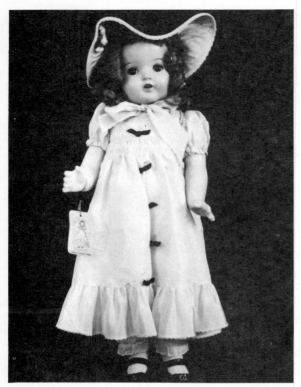

24″ "Princess." All composition, open mouth, four teeth. All original yellow taffeta trimmed in black velvet. Black velvet bonnet lined with yellow taffeta. Blonde human hair wig, blue sleep eyes. Wrist tag: EVERY LITTLE GIRL'S DREAM COME TRUE. "PRINCESS" A MADAME ALEXANDER CREATION. Unmarked. 1937. (Courtesy Martha Sweeney)

9″ "China" of 1938. All composition with painted blue eyes, black wig and all original in multi-color slacks and blue cotton top. Red sash tie, side-snap shoes, three daisies in hair. The 1939 7″ China used the same materials but with the slacks solid color and the top multi-color. Gold paper tag: AN ALEXANDER PRODUCT/SUPREME QUALITY AND DESIGN. Other side: CREATED BY MADAME ALEXANDER. NEW YORK. Tag on top: MADAME ALEXANDER/NEW YORK U.S.A. Body: WENDY ANN/MME ALEXANDER/NEW YORK. (Author)

11″ "Madelaine Du Bain." All composition, brown eyes with gray eyeshadow. All original in flowered and blue striped dress, attached hoop slip, and original box that is blue with imprinted bows. Uses the Wendy Ann doll. Made in 1937-1938 for F.A.O. Schwarz. Tag: MADELAINE, MADAME ALEXANDER N.Y.U.S.A. ALL RIGHTS RESERVED. Has "banana" curls from top of head to shoulders. (Courtesy Nancy Catlin)

1" "Three Pigs." All composition and all original. Marks: MADAME ALEXANDER, on backs. Each wears felt gloves tied t wrist with black ties. Painted features. Each has black and white felt "shoes." Left: pink short pants, black top and all white ap. Middle: pink short pants, blue top and white cap with black rim. Right: blue overalls and billed white cap. 1938. (Courtesy Martha Silva)

11" "Wendy Ann." All composition with brown eyes, human hair blonde wig, swivel waist and all original riding habit, except cap is missing. 1937-1938. Horse is carved wood hand crafted in the 1890's. (Author)

3" "Snow White." All composition with sleep eyes and closed mouth. Black human hair wig and four painted shes at sides of eyes. All original in pink and black. Head marked: PRINCESS ELIZABETH/ALEXANDER DOLL O. Tag: SNOW WHITE (in large letters)/MADAME ALEXANDER N.Y./ALL RIGHTS RESERVED. 1938. (Courtesy Mrs. Richard Hodge)

21″ "Sonja Henie." All composition and completely original in red velvet two piece outfit with rabbit trim, matching cap and white skates. Has original Sonja skate button. (Courtesy Ann Wencel)

18″ "Sonja Henie." All composition and original in black velvet dress with gold sequin heart on bodice and skirt. Original skates are gold. Has original Sonja Skate pin. (Courtesy Ann Wencel)

15″ "Sonja Henie." All composition and original in red velvet trimmed in gold sequins. Has matching cap. The original skates are gold. (Courtesy Ann Wencel)

24″ Marked: PRINCESS ELIZABETH/ALEX. FLOWERGIRL, with reddish brown mohair wig, blue sleep eyes and in original pink taffeta gown with net overlay, white cotton slip and panties, imitation leather shoes. Holds Depression glass basket of roses. ca. 1945. (Courtesy Glorya Woods)

21″ "Margaret O'Brien." All composition and all original in blue dress with white lace and bodice, with two rows of rosettes across bodice. Replaced shoes and socks. Dress is tagged. 1946-1947. (Courtesy Marth Sweeney)

14″ "Babs the Skater." All hard plastic and uses the Margaret O'Brien doll. Blonde mohair wig, blue sleep eyes and dressed in blue with blue fur trim and matching bonnet. Gold skates. Shown with her is a 17″ all original "Sonja Henie" in white with white fur. Blonde hair still in original curls. Sonja is 1940, and the Babs is from 1949. (Courtesy Mary Williams)

20″ "Maggie," all hard plastic, glued on wig, sleep eyes, and original clothes. Red taffeta skirt, white blouse with slip. Tag: MADAME ALEXANDER. 1951 (Courtesy Jeannie Mauldin)

This is the "Godey Group" of 1949-1950. All hard plastic, 14". Back row: pale pink with lace trim, pale blonde with flowers on sides; dark green with trim of fur around bonnet; rose taffeta with white bodice and lace inside matching bonnet; pink with black bodice and lace trim, white lace inside bonnet. Front row: Groom has grey pants with black stripe, Bride is missing her veil. All have floss wigs. (Courtesy Mary Williams)

17½" "Polly Pigtails" or "Kathy" of 1951-1952. All hard plastic using the Maggie face doll. Blue sleep eyes and floss wig. Red head band, body suit and flared dark purple skirt. Tagged: MME. ALEXANDER. Carries a hat box marked MADAME ALEXANDER, on cover. Has a gold medal of the Fashion Academy Award attached. Inside the hat box is comb and curlers. (Courtesy Ann Wencel)

15" "Treena Ballerina" of 1952. All hard plastic with floss wig that is red-orange. The Maggie face doll was also used with this outfit and wig.

15″ "Miss Flora McFlimsey." Hard plastic with vinyl head and has inset (non-moving) eyes. Original pink skirt, white bodice with black front bow, belt and shoes and hose. Straw hat is a replacement. 1952-1953. (Courtesy Sally Bethscheider)

14″ "Peter Pan" (Maggie face). All hard plastic with reddish saran (Newtex) short wig, sleep blue eyes. Brown cotton leotards, green felt shirt, black "leather" belt with silver buckle and brown soft leather boots. Felt hat with green feather. Tag: MADAME ALEXANDER/ALL RIGHTS RESERVED NEW YORK, U.S.A. 1953. (Author)

14″ "Scarlett" (Maggie face). All hard plastic, black side part mohair wig set in curls around head and green sleep eyes. Lace and ribbon trimmed pantaloons and black tie leather shoes. Cotton wired hoop half slip attached to flowered satin gown with black velvet ribbon trim. Inset open weave cotton yoke with wide lace trim. Soft horse-hair straw type hat with roses. 1953. (Author)

8″ "Agatha" of 1953, straight leg non-walker. Black velvet jacket, dark green cotton gown with red flowers. Straw and velvet bonnet with feathers. (Courtesy Bernice Heister)

7¼″ "Quiz-kin" Bride and Groom of 1953-1954. He has molded, painted light brown hair. They have buttons in back that make the head go up and down, or side to side. Both are original and tagged: ALEXANDER-KINS/MADAME ALEXANDER/NEW YORK, N.Y. U.S.A. (Courtesy Nancy Catlin)

Straight leg walker in tagged ALEXANDERKINS blue gabardine coat lined in white. Blue straw hat with flowers and veil. Pink organdy dress. 1955. (Courtesy Bernice Heister)

Wendy 1954-1955 straight leg walker, tagged: ALEXANDERKINS. Navy pleated cotton dress, white felt jacket and hat with red pom-pom. Wendy #468-1955, straight leg walker, tagged: ALEXANDERKIN. Red plaid dress, white felt jacket, white beanie with red pom-poms. (Courtesy Bernice Heister)

1954 "Little Southern Girl." Straight leg, non-walker that is tagged: ALEXANDERKINS. Pink organdy gown and pantaloons, pink satin slippers, straw bonnet and bag with flowers. (Courtesy Bernice Heister)

1954 straight leg walker, tagged: ALEXANDERKIN. Called "Victoria." Black velvet bodice, net sleeves, green and white striped skirt with black, green and pink trim. Black straw hat with flowers. (Courtesy Bernice Heister)

Straight leg walker of 1954-1955. Tagged: ALEXANDERKIN. White organdy blouse and rose taffeta jumper and matching poke bonnet. (Courtesy Bernice Heister)

"Wendy" a straight leg, non-walker; tagged: ALEXANDERKINS. Pink cotton body suit with flowered jumper and pink poke bonnet. 1954. (Courtesy Bernice Heister)

"Wendy" straight leg, non-walker 1954, tagged ALEXANDERKINS blue organdy dress and pink jumper, pink socks, blue shoes. (Courtesy Bernice Heister)

Wendy #450-1955 thru 1957 (#395) straight leg walker, tagged: ALEXANDERKIN. Straw hat, aqua cotton dress, pink & white check pinafore. (Courtesy Bernice Heister)

Straight leg walker. 1955. Tagged: ALEXANDERKIN. Red body suit, white car coat and slacks and hat. All lined in red. (Courtesy Bernice Heister)

1954 "Queen," straight leg walker, tagged: ALEXANDERKIN. White brocade gown, purple cape with "ermine." Jeweled crown. (Courtesy Bernice Heister)

"Dude Ranch" straight leg walker, tagged: ALEX-ANDERKIN. Straw hat with beads and felt, yellow, with fine white stripes, shirt, denim pedal pusher with red trim, brown boots. 1955. (Courtesy Bernice Heister)

8″ Straight leg walker, all original and dressed in white organdy with red rick-rack, red shoes, white straw hat with red berries. Tag: ALEXANDER-KINS. #447-1955 "Tea Party At Grandma's." (Courtesy Linda Crowsey)

8″ Bend knee walker in deep green polished cotton dress with pink collar and inset on bodice. Tag: ALEXANDER-KINS. #585-1956 "Hot Morning." (Courtesy Linda Crowsey)

15″ "Bride" (Margaret) and "Bridesmaids" (Binnie). All hard plastic with wigs and sleep eyes. All three are from 1955. "Bride" in white taffeta and overskirt caught up with flowers. The veil is nylon tulle and attached to bonnet style brim. Left "Bridesmaid" is all pink with nylon tulle trimmed with flowers and over taffeta gown with hoop slip. Flowers in hair. Right is in chartreuse. "Bride" has gold slippers and "Bridesmaids" have silver. "Bride" has straight legs and "Bridesmaids" have joints above the knees and large hands. (Courtesy Elinore Bibby)

"Little Godey" 1955 #491. Tag: ALEXANDERKINS. Chartreuse gown, black beaded felt jacket and felt hat with cutouts and feather and flowers. (Courtesy Bernice Heister)

"Juliet" 1955-#473 straight leg walker, tagged: ALEXANDERKIN. White brocade gown and overdress trimmed in rose velvet with gold crown. "Romeo" #474-1955 straight leg walker, tagged: ALEXANDERKIN. Black jacket and hat trimmed in gold, purple leotards and gold boots. (Courtesy Bernice Heister)

"Bo Peep," straight leg walker #489-1955, tagged: ALEXANDERKIN. Pale pink taffeta dress with rose and green print side panniers and black trim. Black waist band, and natural straw bonnet. (Courtesy Bernice Heister)

"Gretel" 1955 #470, straight leg walker, tagged: ALEX-ANDERKIN. Pink taffeta dress with white organdy top. Black vest, white with blue apron and hat. "Hansel" #445-1955 straight leg walker, tagged: ALEXANDERKIN. One piece combinet shirt and striped leotards. Black pants, white tam. Hat is Alexander, but may not be original to this outfit. (Courtesy Bernice Heister)

1955 "Alice in Wonderland" straight leg walker, tagged: ALEXANDERKINS. Blue taffeta dress and eyelet apron, blue bow in hair. (Courtesy Bernice Heister)

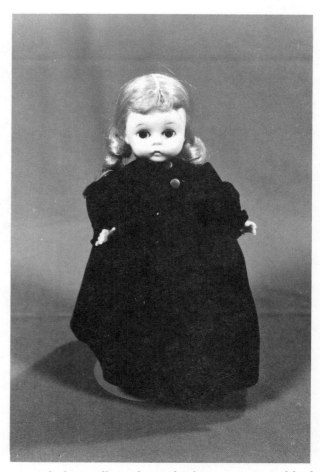

20″ "Cissy Secretary." All original with black lace one piece chemise (tagged), black velvet skirt, white blouse with black and gold tie and white glasses with roses. Black strap pumps with red roses. Same year as "Cissy Walks Her Dog." 1956.

8″ straight leg walker Alexander-kin ca. 1956. In black graduation gown. The cap with tassel is missing.

31

8″ "Southern Belle" in 1956 outfit that is tagged: ALEXANDER-KINS/BY MADAME ALEXANDER. Straight leg walker. The gown is blue and white striped with white trim. (Courtesy Sally Bethscheider)

8″ "Alexander-kin" that is a bend knee walker dressed in a navy blue organdy dress with white polka dots, red trim on bodice and sleeves and a blue band that goes from one sleeve across neck to other sleeve. Replaced shoes and socks. 1956. (Courtesy Sally Bethschieder)

Bend knee walker, tagged: ALEXANDERKIN. Pink and white cotton check romper suit, skirt and poke bonnet of same material. 1956. (Courtesy Bernice Heister)

Bend knee walker, tagged: ALEXANDERKIN, in Beach outfit. White cotton sun hat and jacket trimmed with blue rick-rack. Blue & white cotton sunsuit with lace trimming. Blue sand pail and blue glasses. 1956. (Courtesy Bernice Heister)

Bend knee walker #574 1956 called "Basque." White cotton pleated dress, blue and white striped button down-the-back sweater, white felt French sailor hat with red pom pom. Matching blue and white striped socks. Right is "First Sailor Dress" #576-1956. Bend knee walker, tagged: ALEXANDERKIN. Navy cotton pleated dress. Navy jacket with red, white and blue trim on collar and sleeves. Red tie. Navy felt sailor hat. (Courtesy Bernice Heister)

8″ "Alexander-kin" ca. 1956. The satin dress is white with green ribbon bow and hem length streamers and the coat and matching cap are dark green velvet with light green cotton lining. (Courtesy June Sloniger)

Wendy "Goes Calling" straight leg walker #586-1956. Tagged: ALEXANDERKIN. White organdy dress with pink bow and straw hat. (Courtesy Bernice Heister)

20″ "Cissy Bride." White satin panties, lace hose, stiff half slip, white strap, heeled shoes with silver plastic soles, white straps with rhinestones in center. Gown has attached cotton slip and two-layer, net overskirts. Lined satin top has imported white/silver trim and long, satin lined-in-net sashes that cross in the back to form train. Doll has red hair, vinyl arms, jointed knees. Wears very large rhinestone bracelet and ring. Veil circle of satin rosettes with wired seed pearls that are interwoven to form crown. Made especially for Abram Straus Company. 1957.

20″ "Cissy Bride" of 1957 in same exact gown as other, but has long white gloves, halo of flowers with two layer veil and carries bridal flowers.

Tagged: ALEXANDERKIN, bend knee walker #359 "Time For School." White straw hat with blue velvet ribbon. Pale blue cotton dress with lace edging and large bow in back. 1957. (Courtesy Bernice Heister)

"Dressed For a Hot Morning." Bend knee walker, tagged: ALEX-ANDERKIN. #338-1957. White cotton sun hat. Red and white striped cotton dress with matching bloomers. Red ribbon at shoulders. White attached belt. (Courtesy Bernice Heister)

Bend knee, tagged: ALEXANDER-KIN #321-1960. White cotton dress with a band of floral print ribbon around bottom. (Courtesy Bernice Heister)

Bend knee walker #676-1964. Pink organdy dress with matching pinafore trimmed with lace. (Courtesy Bernice Heister)

"Maggie Mix-up" 1961-#610. Maggie Mixup came with both the "Maggie" face and the "Wendy", as this one is. Blue eyes, freckles, denim overalls with pink and white cotton blouse, pink watering can and pink sandals. Tagged: MAGGIE. (Courtesy Bernice Heister)

8" "India." The doll on the left has a dark red spot on forehead and one on right has a brown spot. Both were purchased in 1980. There are also white skin tone India dolls. (Courtesy Renie Culp)

10″ "Cissette" with tiny blue stone earrings and wearing white brocade gown with gold trim and deep rose taffeta cape. Tag: MADAME ALEXANDER. #977-1957. (Courtesy Linda Crowsey)

10″ "Cissette Bridesmaid" #960-1957. Pink with pink dotted swiss over and sleeves, pink hat with pink roses on sides. Pink sash with pink flowers on skirt and at waist. Pearl earrings. (Courtesy Linda Crowsey)

10″ "Cissette-Lady Hamilton" #975-1957. Pink satin with pink roses on skirt and center of cape-like collar. Pink flowers also on wide brimmed straw hat. (Courtesy Linda Crowsey)

8″ Bend knee walker in blue floral print bathing suit and matching skirt, blue sandals, white straw hat, red glasses. Tag: ALEXANDER-KINS. #520-1958. "Cabana." (Courtesy Linda Crowsey)

8" Bend knee walker in pink pegnoir set. Madame Alexander bed with "brass" finish, red satin headboard, pillow and spread that is trimmed in gold. Pegnoir set tagged: MADAME ALEXANDER NEW YORK. ALL RIGHTS RESERVED. (Courtesy Linda Crowsy)

8" Bend knee walker wearing a pink with blue dotted blouse and blue jumper. Unusual hairdo parted on side and pulled to back. Tag: ALEXANDER-KIN. #365-1959, "May Day." (Courtesy Linda Crowsey)

8" Bend knee walker in hot pink polished cotton dress trimmed in lace with tag: WENDY-KIN. #0431-1963. (Courtesy Linda Crowsey)

10" Red head "Cissette" in pink dotted swiss with satin ribbon tagged: "Cissette." Dressing table with stool covered in red satin and matches bed. (Courtesy Linda Crowsey)

8″ 1981 version of the Limited "Enchanted Doll" has an eyelet cotton pinafore, otherwise is the same as the 1980 doll. 3423 were made in 1981. (Courtesy Shirley Merrill)

8″ "Enchanted Doll" made for the Enchanted Doll House of Manchester, Vermont. Limited to 3000, this is one of the 1980 issue with lace ruffle trim around pinafore and pinafore is made of plain white cotton.

8″ Alexander-kin shown dressed in the 1983 Madame Alexander Convention outfit. Came with certificate calling her "Fairy Queen" and tag on dress reads: ONCE UPON A TIME—FAIRY GODMOTHER". Costume created for the convention by Judy LaManna. limited to 325 outfits. White with pink sash and came with silver trim or blue and pink trim. The pin on front is the souvenir pin from the same convention.

7½″ "Little" Genuis. Soft vinyl arms, legs and body with hard plastic head. Blonde caracul wig. Open mouth/nurser. Blue sleep eyes/molded lashes. Lace trimmed diaper and bonnet. Knit booties, sleeveless slip, organdy eyelet Christening gown. Has glass bottle with Teddy Bear embossed and rubber nipple. Doll not marked. Gown tag: "LITTLE GENUIS"/BY MADAME ALEXANDER/REG. U.S. PAT. OFF. N.Y. 1957. (Courtesy Donnie Durant)

A close up of the 34″-36″ 1952-1953 "Barbara Jane-Penny" face. The eyes are painted and she has a very sweet expression. The child holding her is just as sweet and her name is Nichole Krattli.

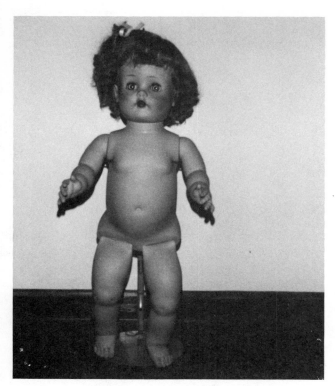

24″ "Bonnie." 1954-1955. All vinyl, rooted hair, sleep blue eyes with heavy stuffed vinyl body and limbs. She is unusual in that the legs fit into the body. Marks: ALEXANDER, on head (Courtesy Jeannie Mauldin)

30″ "Mimi." Hard plastic arms, legs and body with vinyl heads and hands. Jointed at wrists, waist and ankles. Marked: ALEXANDER 1961 on head and original clothes are tagged: MIMI MADAME ALEXANDER. Sleep, flirty eyes with long lashes. Wears pantaloons, panty hose and black shoes. This gown came in pink and in white. (Courtesy Jeannie Mauldin)

Back row: Left: "Scarlett" of 1965 in green satin, white wide lace trim and straw hat with flowers. Right: "Godey" of 1965. The catalogs show the 1965 "Godey," with blonde hair. The gown is red with white lace inside the red bonnet and rows that are vertical on the bodice and on the sleeves. Eyes are brown. Front: "Scarlett" of 1970. Green gown with white trim and lace at sleeve edges. (Courtesy Mary Williams)

The 21″ "Bride" on the left is from the Portrait series of 1965. The darker line around skirt is just a shadow. The other doll is 21″ "Jacqueline" 1962. In white brocade with hot pink draped panniers. (Courtesy Mary Williams)

21″ "Southern Belle" of 1965. Has elaborate hairdo with three sequined chains over front of hairdo and vertical rolls of curls to neckline in back. The gown is turqoise blue with pink flowers at waist and on skirt. (Courtesy Mary Williams)

21″ 1966 "Coco Lissy," one is a blonde and the other has light red hair. Pale pink gowns. (Courtesy Mary Williams)

21″ "Coco" as 1966 "Godey." Black bonnet and short coat and red gown. (Courtesy Sherry Miller)

21″ "Agatha" of 1975 is on the left with white trim on her blue gown and matching bonnet. Right is the 1974 "Cornelia" with black trim on blue gown and bonnet. (Courtesy Mary Williams)

The 21″ "Bride" is from 1969 and the other doll is the 1965 "Renoir" in pink with pink hat, white bodice and lace at sleeves. (Courtesy Mary Williams)

21″ and 11″ "Jenny Lind" dolls of 1969. Both have flowers in hairdo and are dressed in pink. Both have lace trim. (Courtesy Mary Williams)

Back left: 21″ 1969 "Renoir" in yellow with wide lace overskirt, large yellow sash tie and yellow hat. Right: "Gainsborough" of 1972 dressed in blue with wide lace overskirt, blue wide bow sash and straw bonnet. Sitting is 21″ "Gainsborough" of 1968 with blue gown, short jacket with lace over blue, blue trim and hat with tie. (Courtesy Mary Williams)

Back row: Left is 21″ "Mimi of 1971 with dark pink full length coat. The gown under it is pale pink with fancy trim. Right is 21″ "Cornilia" of 1972 with full length pink coat. Gown under it is same pink with fancy trim. Sitting is 21″ 1977 "Magnolia" in pale pink with rows of lace across the front and pink horsehair weave hat with pink ties and flowers. (Courtesy Mary Williams)

Left: 1971 "Godey" in pink with black trim, short jacket and bonnet. Right is 1972 "Renoir" also in pink with black jacket with gold trim, pink hat. In front is a 1972 "Gainsborough" with outfit that has faded to a pale lavender. It was originally blue. (Courtesy Mary Williams)

Back row: Left: 21″ "Melanie" of 1974 with red short jacket and bonnet hat and gown of white. Right is the 1970 "Melanie" dressed in all white with red ribbon trim on skirt, bodice and carries a red umbrella. Sitting is 21″ "Melanie" of 1967 dressed in blue with white trim and bonnet. (Courtesy Mary Williams)

21″ 1970 ''Madame Pompadour'' in pink, blonde hair in a very elaborate hairdo. (Courtesy Mary Williams)

21″ ''Renoir'' of 1973 in golden yellow gown, straw hat with flowers with black ties. (Courtesy Mary Williams)

Back left: ''Elise'' of 1965 in pink and was also available in blue. Center: 16½″ ''Elise'' of 1959 that is hard plastic with vinyl arms, dressed in gold with flower headpiece. Right: 1979-1980 ''Elise'' in blue, (was also available in pink). Front left: unknown Maggie-face hard plastic. Right: 1952 ''Treena Ballerina.'' Margaret face all hard plastic dressed in white with pink flowers. (Courtesy Mary Williams)

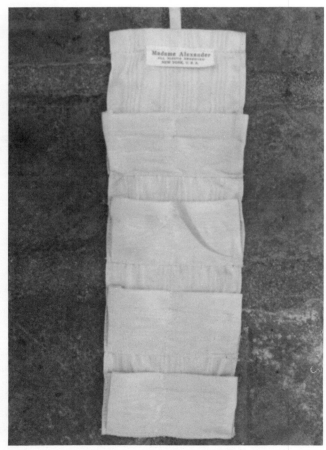 

This pink doll's shoe organizer was made by Madame Alexander and is so tagged. It holds four to eight pairs of shoes. (Courtesy Mimi Hiscox)

15″ ''Caroline'' doll with side part boy's hairdo. These were purchased nude from the Alexander factory by a New York firm and sold to collectors. The doll is referred to as ''John-John,'' but this name is totally without foundation. Here dressed in two ''John-John'' outfits (not tagged and made especially for these dolls). (Courtesy June Schultz)

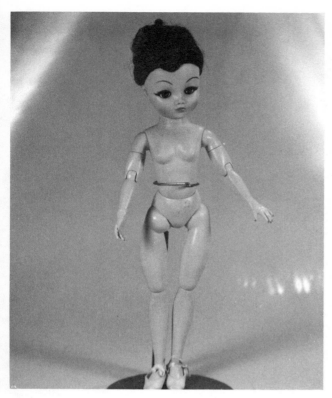

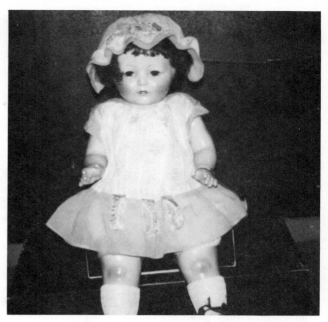

21″ with marks: PETITE AM. CHARACTER DOLL CO., on composition shoulder plate. Composition arms and very fat legs. Original dress is white with blue over shoulders, skirt, and trim on white hat. Yellow insets in skirt and around brim of hat. 1929. (Courtesy Jeannie Mauldin)

21″ "Dollikin" type with all hard plastic body and limbs. Extra joints at ankles, knees and elbows, plus full rotation of arms above the elbows. Waist is "ball" jointed. Vinyl head with black rooted hair in "widow's peak" hair style. Sleep eyes with heavy painted lashes. Marks: KT, on head. Box: MADE BY ALLIED DOLL CO.

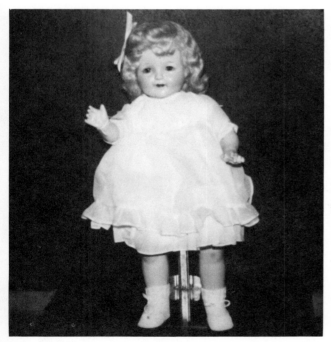

21″ "Toddle-Tot." Came in 18″, 21″ and 24″. Cloth body, composition arms, legs and head. Has slight cheek dimples, sleep eyes and open mouth with molded tongue and upper teeth. Arms are disc jointed. Marks: PETITE, AMER. CHAR. DOLL. CO. on shoulder plate. 1930. (Courtesy Jeannie Mauldin)

15″ Marked: PETITE/AMER. CHAR. Tin blue sleep eyes, composition shoulder plate head, cloth body, composition arms and legs. Mohair wig. Open/closed mouth with two tiny painted upper teeth, cheek dimples. Green dress and hat. All fingers are curled. ca. 1930-1935. (Courtesy Glorya Woods)

 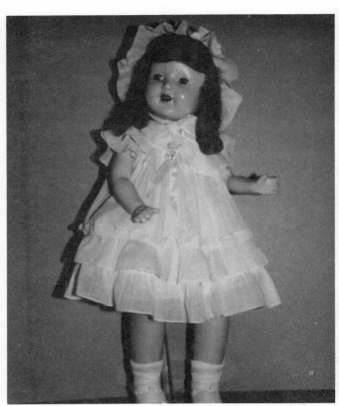

24″ "Perfect Beauty," composition shoulder plates, human hair wigs, cloth bodies, composition arms and legs and open mouth with teeth. All have sleep eyes, but one on left has blue and other two have brown. The doll on the far left is marked: PETITE and dressed in pink organdy with rosette trim. Middle is in light blue organdy and matching bonnet. She is marked: AMER. CHAR. PETITE. 1930-1937. Right is in original pink organdy dress and bonnet to match, white imitation leather shoes. Has cry box in cloth body. (Courtesy Glorya Woods)

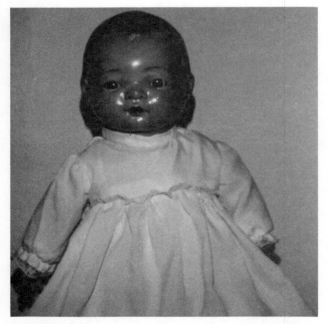

18″ Bye-lo-type "Newborn" Infant. Composition head and hands, cloth body, arms and legs. Molded hair, sleep brown eyes, and marked: AM. CHAR. DOLL, on neck. This same mold was used in vinyl that is marked: AMERICAN CHARACTER DOLL/1958 on head. Has all vinyl body and limbs, and also came a year later with plastic body and limbs. (Courtesy Jeannie Mauldin)

14″ "Baby Sue." Cloth bodies, vinyl arms and legs, hard plastic heads. One has molded hair and other has wig over molded hair. Sleep eyes, closed mouth, marked: AMERICAN CHARACTER on heads. 1950-1951. The earlier ones had "magic skin" bodies and limbs. The later ones were of all vinyl. (Courtesy Jeannie Mauldin)

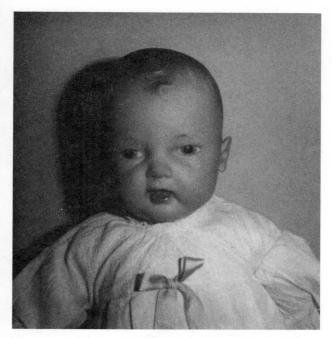

16″ Beautiful baby with vinyl head, arms and legs, cloth body. Molded hair, open/closed mouth, marked: AM. CHAR. DOLL on head. The eyes are painted blue and the doll has very nice modeling. ca. 1953. (Courtesy Jeannie Mauldin)

Group of cloth bodied babies with vinyl heads and limbs, from various companies. All have painted eyes, most have frowning, crying style face modeling. Back, left to right: Madame Alexander, Effanbee, Horseman, and in front: American Character and Arranbee. (Courtesy Jeannie Mauldin)

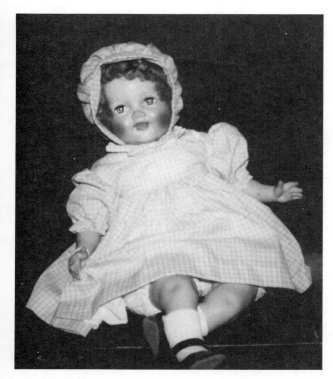

24″ "Chuckles" of 1955. This doll also used as the "Baby Sue." Cloth body with vinyl head and limbs. Rooted hair, sleep blue eyes and open/closed mouth with two upper teeth. Marks: AMER. CHAR. DOLL on head. Re-dressed. (Courtesy Jeannie Mauldin)

16″ "Chuckles" of 1958 using the "Ricky, Jr." mold. Where the "Ricky Jr." doll had molded hair, this one has rooted hair over the molded. Has open/closed mouth with molded tongue and is all vinyl. Sleep blue eyes. Dress is white with lace and net trim and she wears a bonnet hat trimmed in lace. (Courtesy Jeannie Mauldin)

14″ "Sweet Sue" that is all hard plastic and in original pink multi lace gown. Sleep eyes and glued-on wig. Head marked: A.C. 1955. (Courtesy June Schultz)

14″ "Sweet Sue Sophisticate." All hard plastic walker with sleep eyes/lashes. Glued-on wig. Sleeves and ribbons have faded from deep rose to purple. Carries hat-type box which is tagged: SWEET SUE'S CHARLES OF THE RITZ CHIGNON. 1956. (Courtesy June Schultz)

25″ "Toni." Same doll as large size "Sweet Sue." All rigid vinyl with vinyl head, rooted hair and sleep eyes. Pierced ears and pale painted nails. Marks: AMER. CHARACTER on head. Tag: TONI BY AMERICAN CHARACTER. Dressed in black bodice and ribbons, dress is red. 1956. (Courtesy Marjorie Uhl)

17″ "Sweet Sue Godey Lady" of 1956. All hard plastic, dark wig pulled to back curls and braids, sleep eyes, green and red plaid gown, deep rose sleeves, collar and ribbons. Walker, head turns. Same gown that is on the 1957 "Sweet Sue Sophisticate."

18″ "Sweet Sue" walker that is hard plastic with vinyl arms. Head turns from side to side. Hair rooted into vinyl skull cap. She wears original party dress of pink organdy, pink sash and has a straw bag tied to wrist with pink ribbon. Straw hat with flowers. Socks are white with pink bands. Jointed at elbows and knees. 1956. (Courtesy Marjorie Uhl)

18″ "Sweet Sue." Hard plastic walker, head turns side to side, has vinyl arms, jointed at elbows and knees. Hair is reddish and rooted into skull cap of vinyl. Sleep eyes and all original in pink organdy, lace trimmed gown with pink satin bodice and rosettes. Straw hat with ring of blue flowers and carries a blue flower. 1956. (Courtesy Marjorie Uhl)

18″ "Sweet Sue." All hard plastic walker with head turning side to side. Green sleep eyes, reddish rooted hair set in vinyl skull cap. Original pink gown with gold trim. 1957. (Courtesy June Schultz)

31″ "Sweet Sue." Vinyl head and arms, with jointed elbows. Rooted hair and sleep eyes. Hard plastic body and legs, with jointed knees. Original dress is pink with white organdy yoke and lower sleeves. White lace trim. 1957. (Courtesy June Schultz)

30″ "Sweet Sue." Hard plastic walker, flat feet and jointed knees. Has vinyl arms with jointed elbows. Brown hair rooted into skull cap, blue sleep eyes, marked: AMERICAN CHARACTER DOLL on head. Cost $19.95 in 1958. (Courtesy Shirley Merrill)

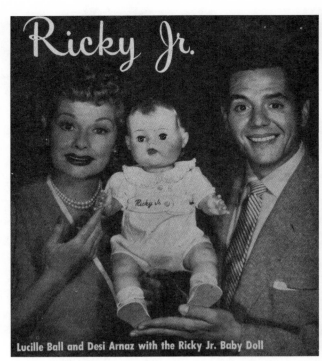

Lucille Ball and Desi Arnaz with the Ricky Jr. Baby Doll

The 1956 "Ricky Jr." doll was 21″ and made of all heavy vinyl. Came with molded as well as rooted hair. Also available was a Playtime Doll Carriage with RICKY JR., in script printed on the side, a trimble bath set with towels that had a heart shaped imprint, also packaged extra clothes. The 21″ 1956 doll sold for $14.98. Also came in 16″ size.

This is the 1955 "I Love Lucy Baby" (prior to the birth of Ricky, Jr.). The doll was also used on the show in place of the real infant. The first ones were offered in 16″ size for $9.98.

25″ "Sweet Sue" marked: AMER CHAR. on head. Vinyl head with rooted hair and sleep eyes. Rigid vinyl body and limbs with jointed waist and ankles. Pink nails and dressed all original in brown straw hat, pink nylon dress with scalloped-trim bottom. Rhinestone bow at neck, stone trim on shoes. (Courtesy Ann Wencel)

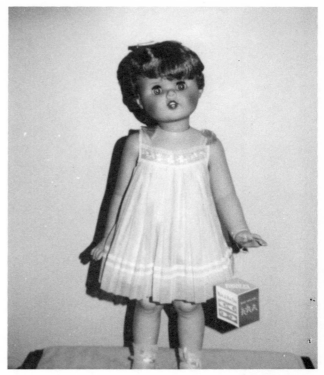

The upswept rooted hairdo on the 24½″ "Sweet Sue." Uses "Toodles" head & body. (Courtesy Jeannie Mauldin)

30″ "Toodles" 1960 walker with plastic body and legs. Vinyl arms and head. Rooted hair, sleep eyes/lashes, called "follow me eyes." Open/closed mouth with four upper and two lower teeth painted in. Tag: TOODLES, PEEK-A-BOO EYES. AMERICAN DOLL & TOY CO. Mint and original. (Courtesy Ann Wencel)

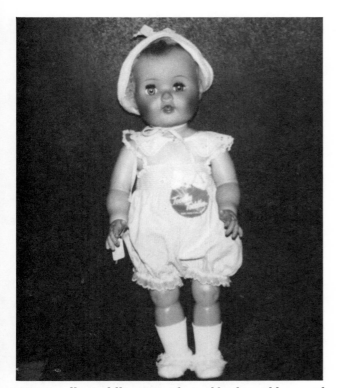

22″ "Toodle Toddler." Rigid vinyl body and legs with vinyl arms and head. Molded hair, flirty sleep eyes with thick, long lashes. Open mouth, slightly bent arms and open hands. Original pink romper suit and hat. Tag: TOODLES TODDLER, WALKS, STANDS AND SITS. Head marked: AMER. CHAR. DOLL CORP. 1960. (Courtesy Jeannie Mauldin)

8″ "Tiny Betsy McCall." All hard plastic, jointed knees and dark brown hair rooted into skull cap (wig), in original clothes. (Courtesy Shirley Merrill)

8″ "Tiny Betsy McCall." Marks: MCCALL CORP. 1958, in circle. All hard plastic with jointed knees, sleep eyes and glued-on wigs. Shown in original box with original chemise. The clothes could be purchased separately, although the dolls were also sold in various outfits. Pleated skirt dress of red with white trim. The lower two were a gift from a very special person: Green Ballerina with pink flowers and ribbons, and blue polka dot dress, white trim and red ribbon. (Author)

21″ All original "Miss Take Whimsie—Betty The Beauty." Original red bathing suit and sandals. Name on yellow ribbon across front as well as on the tag. Green plastic sun glasses, earrings, bracelet and hair holders in yellow-gold. Marks: WHIMSIES 1960 AMER. DOLL & TOY., circle. Black rooted hair. (Courtesy Jeannie Mauldin)

21″ "Dixie the Pixie." All one piece stuffed vinyl body and limbs. Blonde curly hair in front and two braids in back. Pink and white check dress with white trim and rosettes. Pink bows in braids and white sandals. Marks: WHIMSIES/1960/AMERICAN DOLL & TOY, in circle on head. (Courtesy Lynette Timmons)

21″ "Fanny The Flapper" Whimsie of 1960. Blonde rooted hair, gold plastic earrings and bracelet, black dress. Marks: WHIMSIES/1960/AMERICAN DOLL & TOY, in circle on head. (Courtesy Lynette Timmons)

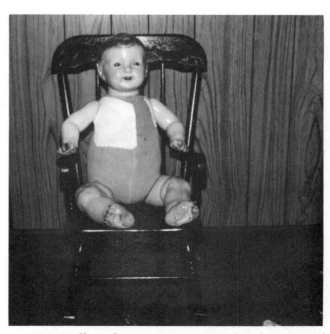

24″ "My Dolly" of 1927. Composition head, arms and legs. Fat, stuffed cloth body (with patches). Deeply molded, painted brown hair, smiling sleep eyes and open mouth. Slightly bent fat baby legs and both molded arms bent at elbows. (Courtesy Jeannie Mauldin)

12″ All composition doll with molded, painted hair and eyes painted straight ahead. Both arms slightly bent at the elbows. She has on an original "Nancy" dress of white with pink trim, but doll is marked "IT", on the back. The doll was made by the Louis Amberg Company in 1932, *but,* it was the practice of doll companies not set up to make their own composition dolls during the early 1930's to purchase dolls from other makers. This same doll was purchased by the Madame Alexander Co. for their doll "Betsy" in 1934 and 1935. This same doll will also be found marked: KEWTY, but with slightly different bangs. (Courtesy Martha Sweeney)

12″ "Sweetie Lue." All composition with jointed shoulders, hips and neck. Marks: ARRANBEE/DOLL CO. 1932, on head. Eyes are painted to the side, has nicely modeled hair. A 12″ doll using same head, but marked "NANCY" (1930-1936), has both arms bent at the elbows. (Courtesy Mrs. Frank Miller)

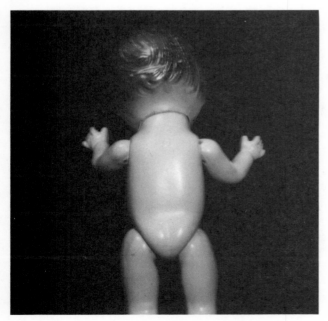

The back view of the marked "IT" doll, so the back side of the hairdo can be seen. Earlier "IT" doll will be marked: AMBERG/PAT PEND./L.A. & S-1928. (Courtesy Martha Sweeney)

14″ Reddish brown molded hair, blue tin sleep eyes, Patsy-type body with elbow bent on one arm. All composition. Marks: KEWTY, on body. Arranbee Patsy look-a-like. Another "Kewty" has same side hair style as this one but has deep side part with bangs swirled sidewards across the forehead. (Courtesy Glorya Woods)

14″ "Dream Baby." Also called "Drink'n Babe." All composition toddler body with molded brown curly hair, sleep brown eyes, open mouth with two upper teeth and dimple in chin. Original yellow organdy dress and bonnet, white cotton lace trim slip, flannel diaper, white imitation leather shoes. 1934-1939. Shown with an 11″ "Dionne Quint" by Madame Alexander, also in yellow organdy tagged dress. (Courtesy Glorya Woods)

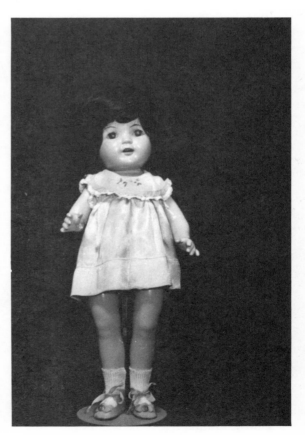

17″ "Nancy." All composition with black human hair wig, large sleep eyes. All original in blue velvet coat and hat. Wears light blue rayon dress, trimmed with flowers on organdy collar. Original shoes and socks. 2nd and 3rd fingers molded together and slightly curled. Marks: NANCY/ARRANBEE. 1936-1937. (Courtesy Martha Sweeney)

20″ "Nancy." All composition with open mouth and four teeth. Marked: NANCY, on head. All original brown velvet coat with hood, fur muff, red leather shoes, wearing a cream color taffeta dress. Buttons on dress are the same as on the coat. Excellent quality clothes and doll. 1939. (Courtesy Martha Sweeney)

17″ "Nancy." All composition with sleep eyes, glued- on wig and open mouth. Original pink organdy dress. 1937. Marks: NANCY, on head. (Courtesy Martha Sweeney)

14″ "Princess Betty Rose" of 1937-1938. Uses the closed mouth version of "Debu-teen" and "Sonja Henie." Doll is unmarked, box is marked: DEBUTEEN. Owner received doll for Christmas 1939. Original pink taffeta gown with pink net, white fur jacket. Blonde human hair wig, brown sleep eyes. (Courtesy Martha Sweeney)

18″ "Nancy Lee." Marked: R&B. Also came in ice skating costume as "Sonja Henie." All composition, blonde mohair wig, brown sleep eyes, dark eyeshadow, closed mouth. Composition came in 14″, 18″ and 21″ sizes; hard plastic 17″. Original flowered taffeta trimmed in blue. Childhood doll of Betty Selby; her twin sister had same doll with blue eyes and same gown trimmed in pink. 1939. (Courtesy Glorya Woods)

25″ "Baby Nancy Lee" by Arranbee. Composition head and limbs with cloth body, blue sleep eyes, open mouth with two upper and two lower teeth. Painted, molded hair. Used until 1939. Ideal doll company also made a doll during the same period that looks very much like this one, called "Sally." (Courtesy Betty Wood)

21″ "Dream Baby," also used as "Baby Nancy" of 1939. Composition head and limbs with cloth body, molded painted blonde hair, blue tin sleep eyes, cheek dimples and open mouth with two upper teeth. All original in pink dress and bonnet trimmed in lace. Dress tag: DREAM BABY/AN ARRANBEE DOLL. Doll is unmarked. 1936-1937. (Courtesy Martha Sweeney)

15″ "Teen" doll marked: R & B on head. These dolls came with cloth bodies and composition head and limbs, as well as all composition. This one has black human hair wig and is being called "Deanna Durbin," but this is without foundation. ca. 1940. Wears original yellow net over satin gown with yellow trim and flowers, straw hat with yellow ribbon tie and gold sandals. (Courtesy Evelyn Samec)

17″ "Nancy." All composition, glued-on wig, sleep eyes and open mouth with two upper teeth and tongue. Marks: NANCY on head. Original "Prom Date" gown of white with pink ribbon trim and a large flower at waist. 1940. (Courtesy Jeannie Mauldin)

17″ Nancy "Southern Girl-1941." All composition with sleep eyes, open mouth with teeth and glued on wig. Gown has hoop slip that is yellow with yellow ribbon trim. Gold sandals. (Courtesy Sally Bethscheider)

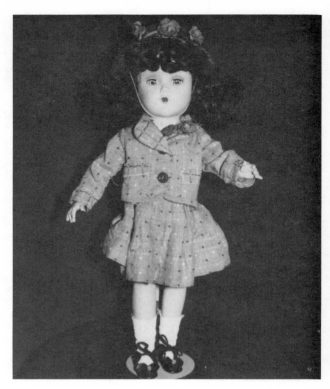

14″ "Nanette." All hard plastic with sleep eyes/lashes. 1953. Original grey two piece suit with red dots, buttons, and roses on lapel and red straw hat. Has two pockets on jacket with red trim. (Courtesy Mary Williams)

14″ "Nanette" of 1955. All hard plastic with glued-on yellow blonde wig. Her original dress is olive green, dark green, red and white plaid skirt with white bodice, red buttons and belt and has "suspenders" which have hearts and say "I love you." (Courtesy Judy Olive)

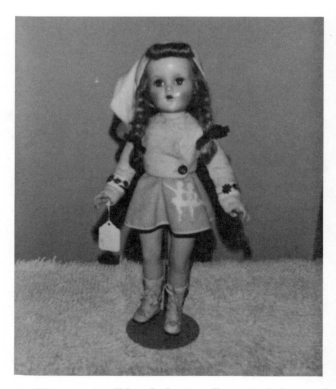

17″ "Nanette." All hard plastic, all original skater of the 1950's. Top is white with sleeves trimmed in red flowers, buttoned at waist. Skirt is blue with white felt applied skaters cutouts. White skates. (Courtesy Ann Wencel)

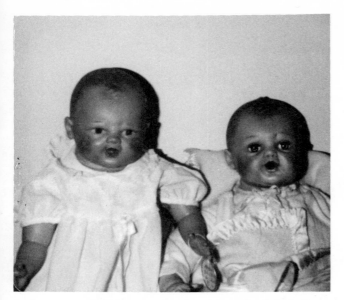

Left: 22″ and right: 19″. Both are marked: R & B, on necks. Both are frowning have molded hair and the left one has painted eyes while the right one has sleep eyes. Both have cloth bodies with vinyl limbs. The right one is all original in pink blanket, diaper, undershirt and gown trimmed in pink ribbon. 1949-1952. (Courtesy Jeannie Mauldin)

12″ "Sweet Angel." All vinyl with blonde rooted hair, blue sleep eyes and marked: R&B on back. Not original clothes. 1957. Called "Little Dear" in 1956. (Courtesy Shirley Merrill)

10″ "Littlest Angel." All hard plastic body with ball; pin jointed hips. Jointed knee walker. Head turns. Viny head with rooted hair and sleep eyes. 1959. This doll was all hard plastic in 1956. Original ballerina costume.

15″ "Bell Doll" with box marked: DESIGNED EXCLUSIVELY FOR TELEPHONE PIONEERS OF AMERICA. Plastic body and legs with vinyl head and limbs. Rooted hair, blue sleep eyes/lashes and blue eyeshadow over eyes. All original including jeans, white shirt with Bell emblem and blue jacket with black belt and orange phone hand set attached. Outfit includes plastic hard hat with company emblems on sides and blue and yellow stripes. Marks: A & H DOLL/1982. Available in Black or White versions.

Emmett Kelly as "Willie, The Clown" in various sizes. Cloth and vinyl with lower left being all vinyl figure and lower third from left, a hand puppet. Tag: EXCLUSIVE LICENCE/BABY BERRY/TOY. N.Y.C., and other side: EMMETT KELLY/WILLIE THE CLOWN.

"Captain Kangaroo" in various sizes. Cloth and vinyl. Can be marked: B.B., on head. Tag: EXCLUSIVE LICENSEE/BABY BERRY/TOY N.Y.C. and on other side: CAPTAIN/KANGAROO. Some will be marked: 1961 ROBT. KEESHAN/ASSOC. INC. on head. All have white molded hair and caps are molded on.

14″ "Ginny Tui," TV personality of 1960's. Plastic body and legs with vinyl arms and head, rooted hair and painted features. Rooted hair is pulled up into twin braided sections high on side and tied with red yarn in two places. Original aqua-green two piece outfit with gold frog closers on top. Embroidered circles of Chinese figures and has white edging on top. Black slippers with white socks. Doll is unmarked, except for 15-5 on lower back. Original box is red with gold circles as are on clothes and states: LOVE ALWAYS/GINNY TUI/THE CHINA DOLL. Made by Jack Built Toys, Burbank, Ca.

The Block Doll Corporation of New York made an all hard plastic walking doll with glued on wigs and sleep eyes in a 10″ and 12″ size. This same doll with same three outfits was also made with a button that went through the doll and when the front is pressed the head shakes "no," and when the back is pressed the head moves "yes," also in the same sizes. The dolls will be unmarked. ca. mid-1950's.

The Block Doll Corporation made an 11″ walker in these three outfits with the one being in a box with extra clothes. This same doll was made in the 14″ size in the check dress and as a Bride but not with box and extra clothes. These dolls have jointed knees, hard plastic body and limbs but have vinyl heads with rooted hair. The dolls will be unmarked. ca. mid-1950's.

17"'Goldilocks." Plastic and vinyl with rooted white hair and sleep eyes, closed mouth smile. Original with blue flowered gown, white apron and combination blue and white bonnet. The apron has her name on it and she wears a charm bracelet with three bears. Tag: GOLDILOCKS/AND HER THREE BEARS. Marks: Brookglad, on head, "1756-G2," on back. (Courtesy Marge Meisinger)

13" Black "Scootles" with black hair, brown side glancing eyes and all original. Red and white stripe cotton romper with blue ruffle at sleeves. Imitation leather shoes, rayon socks. Gold wrist tag: "SCOOTLES" DESIGNED & COPYRIGHT BY ROSE O'NEILL. A CAMEO DOLL. 1930's Shown with a 12" J. D. Kestner mold 221, googly with bisque head and composition jointed body. (Courtesy Glorya Woods)

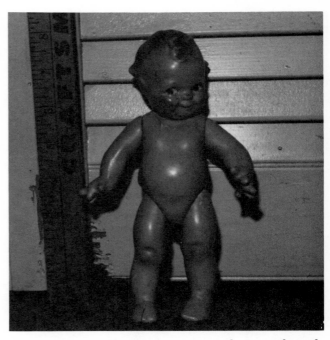

13" "Scootles" jointed at neck, shoulders and hips. Blonde sculptured hair, eyes painted to the front. Maybe original dress. Shown with Scootle-faced cookie jar lid with molded Davy Crockett style hat and top of clothes. 1930's (Courtesy Glorya Woods)

8" "Scootles". All composition with jointed neck, shoulders and hips, sculptured hair and eyes painted to the sides. Unmarked. 1930's (Courtesy Jackie Barker)

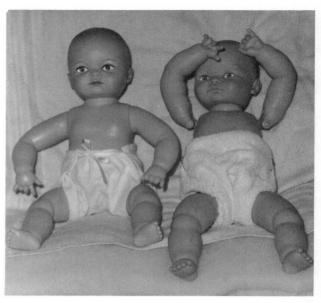

18″ "Plum" 1952-54. All vinyl with rooted hair, sleep eyes, dimples in cheeks and chin. Has hinged jointed body like some Kewpies and Miss Peep. Marks: CAMEO, on head and body. (Courtesy Shirley Merrill)

The newer "Miss Peep" dolls, on the market in the 1970's and 1980's, are jointed at shoulders and hips, as shown on the left. The doll on the right is the older 1950's "Miss Peep" with pin jointed shoulders and hips. Both have molded hair and inset blue eyes. (Courtesy Phyllis Teague)

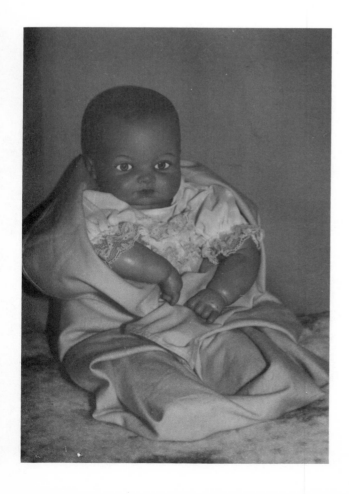

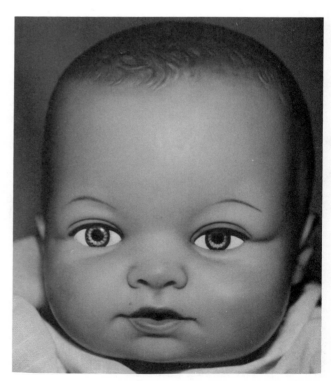

This older "Miss Peep" is 17″ tall with inset blue eyes, is a nurser/open mouth Drink-and-Wet baby. She has the pin hinged joints at shoulders and hips. Head and body are marked: CAMEO. 1957. (Courtesy Phyllis Teague)

15" Black "Miss Peep" with hinged joints at shoulders and hips. Inset brown eyes and has Cameo tag. Marks: CAMEO, on head and body. All original. 1957. (Courtesy Kathy Feagans)

This 19" older "Miss Peep" has the pin jointed shoulders and hips, molded hair and inset *brown* eyes. (Courtesy Phyllis Teague)

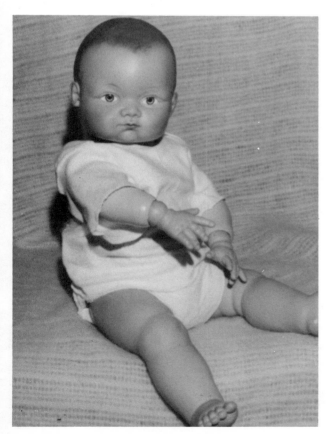

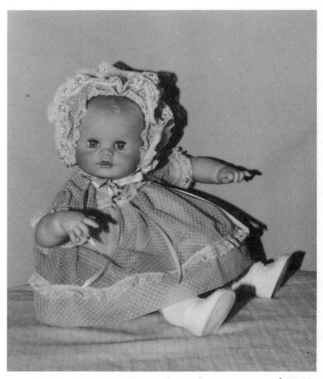

19" "Newborn Miss Peeps." Plastic body and arms with vinyl hands, head and legs. Jointed wrists, molded hair and brown inset eyes. Marked: CAMEO. 1962. (Courtesy Phyllis Teague)

19" "Baby Mine." All vinyl on the pin jointed "Miss Peep" body. Has sleep eyes, molded tongue and molded hair. Clothes made by Shirley Pully. 1962. (Courtesy Phyllis Teague)

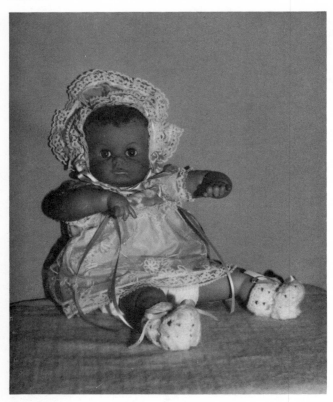

19″ Sleep eyes "Baby Mine" with rooted, very short, reddish-brown hair. On the "Miss Peep" pin hinged body. Clothes by Shirley Pully. 1962. (Courtesy Phyllis Teague)

10″ and 6″ "Kewpies." Stuffed red plush bodies with vinyl faces, made in a sitting position. Small doll has blue painted eyes and the larger one has black painted eyes. Both tagged: KNICKERBOCHER TOY CO. INC/NEW YORK U.S.A./KEWPIE/DESIGNED & COPYRIGHT/BY ROSE O'NEILL/LICENSED BY CAMEO DOLL CO. 1964. (Courtesy Ruth Anderson)

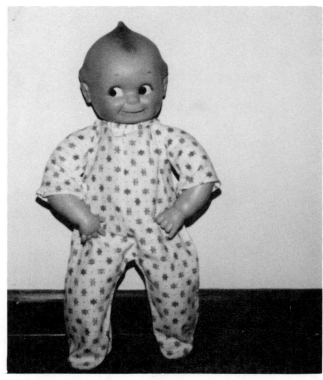

10″ "Ragsy Kewpie." Jointed at neck only. Body is one piece blue vinyl, head is vinyl with blue bonnet, painted features and hair. Marks: CAMEO 65 JLK, on head and CAMEO 65, on body. 1964. Childhood toy of Brent Merrill.

18″ "Kewpie." All vinyl, on the "Miss Peep" body with pin hinged limbs. Painted features and original one-piece pajamas. Marks: CAMEO on head and body. Has: "SI/61C2/63," on doll's bottom. ca. 1960's. (Courtesy Jeannie Mauldin)

These are the Kewpies made by the Jesco Imports, Inc. They are from the original 1950's Cameo molds. The largest is 27". Introduced in 1983.

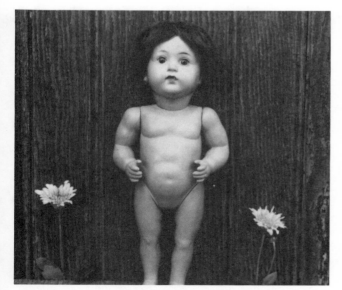

8" all celluloid on a small toddler body. Glued on wig and inset glass eyes, 2nd and 3rd fingers slightly curled into palms. Marks: HELMET MARK/2, on head and HELMET MARK/25 GERMANY 26½, on back. The Helmet mark: are dolls made by the Minerva firm of A. Vischer Co in U.S. and Buschow & Beck of Germany. ca. 1920's (Courtesy Kay Bransky)

7" celluloid head and body with stuffed arms and legs. Molded pale yellow hair, painted eyes and original clothes. Carriage is marked: MADE IN PORTUGAL. The doll is unmarked. (Courtesy Betty Wood)

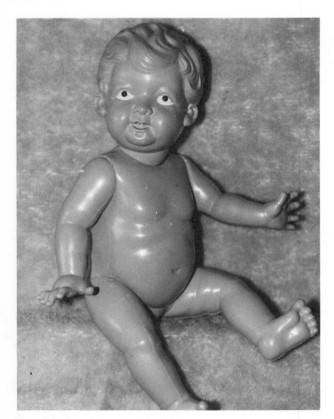

26″ Large all celluloid baby with painted eyes, open/closed mouth and two upper teeth with molded tongue. Modeled hair painted yellow and marked:      MADE IN JAPAN 2, on back. (Courtesy Shirley Merrill)

12″ celluloid boy that is jointed at neck, shoulders and hips, painted grey eyes, modeled hair that is painted red, marked: JAPAN, on the back. This doll has been called "Prince Charles," but there certainly is no foundation for this name. (Courtesy Shirley Merrill)

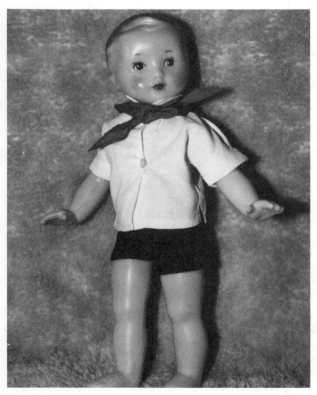

14″ boy that is all celluloid with painted eyes and molded hair. In original clothes, but missing shoes and socks. Unmarked. (Courtesy Freda Webster)

8″ Celluloid girl with painted features, molded brown hair with molded bow. Marked: IRWIN, on back. Made in early 1940's and given to owner by her grandmother. (Courtesy Shirley Merrill)

8″ Celluloid baby, fully jointed with painted features, molded hair and marked: NON-FLAM, on back of head. Maker unknown. (Courtesy Shirley Merrill)

12″ "Lady from Brittany." Made in France. All celluloid doll with one piece body and head, jointed at shoulders and hips. Painted blue eyes, glued-on wig, has excellent detail to hands and costume. Made in 1930's. (Courtesy Betty Woods)

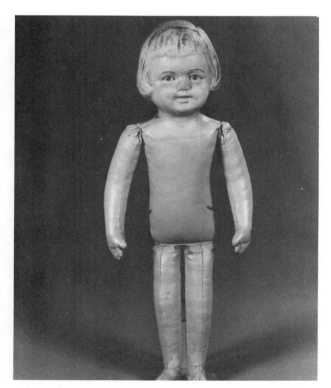

16″ Chase doll of the late 1930's, 1940's or 1950's. All "oil cloth" style material with material hardened for the head. Molded hair and oil painted features. Free standing thumb and stitched fingers and toes. The early Chase dolls (1920's) are "jointed," by stitching, at the knees and the elbows. (Courtesy Jayn Allen)

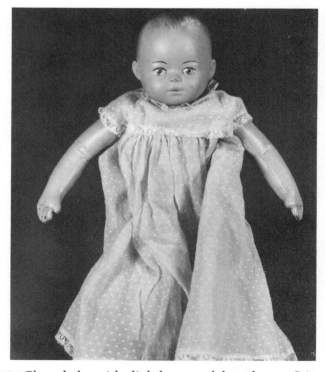

16″ Chase baby with slightly curved, bent knees. Stitched fingers. Lightly molded hair that is brush painted. Oil painted features. Dates from 1940's-1950's. (Courtesy Jayn Allen)

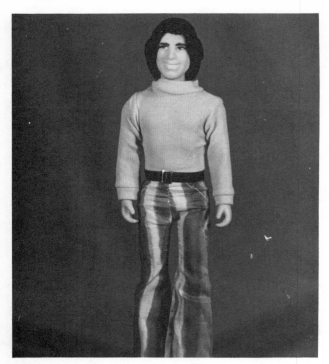

11½″ "John Travolta." All plastic with vinyl arms and head. Extra joints at waist and knees only. Molded black hair, painted blue eyes and open/closed mouth with painted white teeth. Marks: 32/HONG KONG, on head. Made by Chemtoy. 1977.

8½″ "Galaxy Maiden." Distributed by City Products Corp. Late 1970's. Doll is not marked. Plastic body and legs with jointed waist. Vinyl arms and head. Rooted hair, painted eyes with three painted lashes at sides of eyes, plus green "V," blue painted eyebrows and has a "lighting bolt" green mark on cheek. Wearing original gold jumpsuit, has gold wrap around skirt in package. White boots. (Courtesy Marie Ernst)

17″ Madame Alexander Dionne Quint marked: DIONNE/ALEXANDER, on head and ALEXANDER, on body. Shown with 17″ Kathe Kruse boy with oil painted features, marked on the right foot: GERMANY, on the left foot: KATHE KRUSE/Jf 89. (Courtesy Glorya Woods)

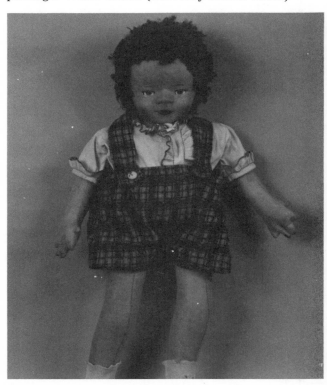

25″ Boy, flesh color cloth seams in middle of legs and sides of arms. 2nd and 3rd fingers stitched together. Painted mask face of felt or velvet, back of head made of cloth. Head molded over hard form. Unmarked.

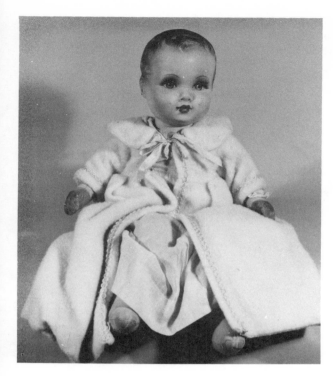

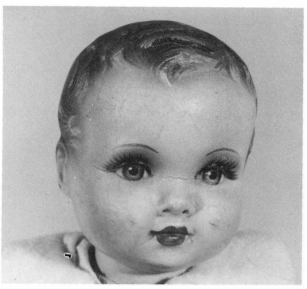

20″ white cotton stuffed body, slightly bent long legs and arms to wrists. Pink velvet hands with stitched fingers. Sewn so "jointed" at shoulder and hips. The beautifully modeled baby head is a jointed socket head. The material of the head is not cloth, but like a composition, or a heavy material with a rubber layer over it. The features are hand painted in oils and the hair is molded and painted. Tag on left foot: MADE IN ENGLAND/BY/DEAN'S RAG BOOK. ca. 1930's.

10″ (sitting). All dark brown felt with fingers and toes stitched and free standing thumbs. Jointed at neck and in original state with chain bracelet, necklace and two drops caught and stitched along with button on center of head piece. Metal hoop earrings are sewn to head piece. Headpiece and top are made of velvet that is orange on one side and grey (may have been white) on other. Cloth lower clothes and has chain around one ankle. Glass inset eyes to side with celluloid glasses, oil painted smiling mouth. Has paper tag: CHAD VALLEY/HYGIENIC TOYS/MADE IN ENGLAND. Sewn on cloth tag on bottom of foot: HYGIENIC TOYS/MADE IN ENGLAND BY/CHAD VALLEY CO. LTD. ca. 1920's or early 1930's.

12″ Tagged: MADE IN ENGLAND. All cloth with cloth back to head and buckram molded front half of head that is highly colored and has oil painted features. Felt ears, mohair wig on base sewn to head. Original clothes and hat that include a "walking halter" strap with bell, which is leatherette. Ties to the bonnet are felt. Three stitched fingers with free formed thumb. Both knees are pulled together and stitched. (Courtesy Jayn Allen)

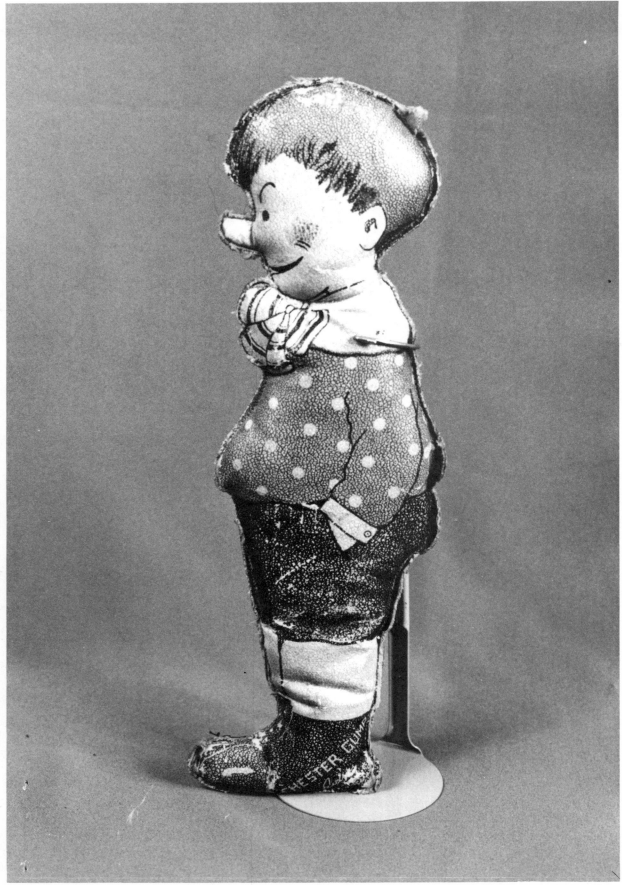

12″ "Chester Gump." All oil painted on heavy canvas and same on both sides. Red hair and shirt, blue short pants. Marks: CHESTER GUMP BY(rest of name unreadable). (Courtesy Kathy Feagans)

14″ "Royal Guard" made by Farnell's Alpha Toys in London, England. All cloth with felt face, oil painted features, stitched fingers. Excellent quality clothing that is not removable. Early 1930's. (Author)

15½″ Felt head with oil painted features and painted hair. Cotton stuffed and covered body and limbs. Excellent quality clothes denoting Scotland. Not tagged. Maker could be either Chad Valley or Norah Welling, both firms located in England. ca. 1930's. (Courtesy Marilyn Hitchcock)

14″ All cloth with printed features, yarn hair and removable pinafore style apron. ca. 1930's. Most likely is a "cut and sew" doll.

17″ Painted stockinette head, applied ears, yarn hair W.P.A. doll of the 1930's. All cloth body. (Courtesy Sally Freeman)

15″ Clown of early 1930's. All stockinette with face that is pressed and molded, non-removable clothes and shoes. Clothes, shoes and fringe are velvet. Tag: KRUEGER N.Y. (Courtesy Jayn Allen)

12″ Plush duck with sewn-on corduroy overalls, removable felt hat. Wears banner: A CHICAGO CENTURY OF PROGRESS 1934. Jointed only at the shoulders. Small tag: GUND ANIMAL. (Courtesy Jayn Allen)

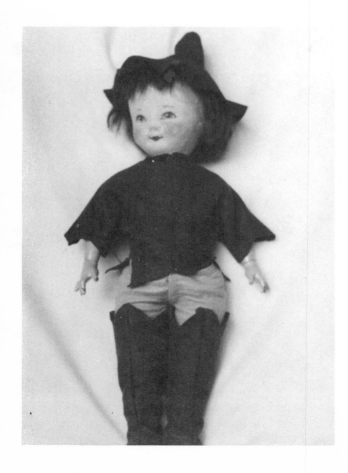

15″ Boy that is very well made with painted features on a mask velvet head. Cloth body, lower arms of wood, fine painted latex hands. Jointed wrists and elbows. Jointed at neck, shoulders and hips. Mohair wig. Felt clothes are not original, but certainly look right on him. (Courtesy Nancy Lucas)

16″ "Little Bo Peep" by Mollye with orange/brown yarn hair, cloth in back of head, and buckram face that is oil painted. All cloth body with thin hands and free standing thumbs. Center stitched legs. Original except large brim bonnet is missing. (Courtesy Jayn Allen)

16″ "Snow White" with mask face with eyes painted to the side, black mohair wig. Oil cloth type arms, cloth body and legs. Not original clothes.

12″ Twins that are all cloth with printed features, hair and under clothes. Dress is a cut-and-sew type as are the dolls. (Courtesy Jayn Allen)

10″ Twins. All cloth with painted features, wood shoes and removable skirt. Yarn braids. Unmarked. (Courtesy Jayn Allen)

10″ Sicilian Peasant Women that is all cloth and all original. Mask face with oil painted features. Has paper tag under apron marked: BULLOCK'S DOLLS FROM MANY LANDS, 1938. (Courtesy Gertrude Smith)

22″ "Little Annie Rooney" type doll from the 1930's comic strip. Soft stuffed, sateen face, torso and limbs are pink/white check cotton, 10½″ legs, yellow yarn braided hair, removable white collar, black/white jumper. Unjointed. (Courtesy Margot Mandel)

17″ Mask face all cloth with marcelled and pulled back hair. Round painted eyes and smile mouth. No finger detail and arms are a sateen material. Heavy canvas/muslin type body and legs with sewn-on navy boots. Original clothes. Attached paper tag: VAN CAMP HARDWARE & IRON CO. INC. INDIANAPOLIS (Courtesy Jayn Allen)

7″ "Puck" with all oil cloth body, seams on sides and down front of body. Velvet red overalls with blue felt buttons and has blue felt base to feet. Pressed, oil painted face, red velvet peaked cap with white felt laps-ears. Mohair is sewn to cap. The back of the head is cloth. Also has white oil cloth collar. Gift from close friend. Tag: KRUEGER N.Y./REG. U.S. PAT. OFF./MADE IN U.S.A.

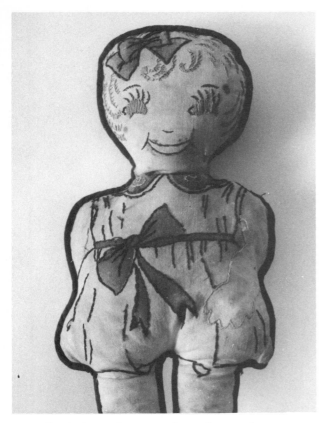

15″ All cloth with painted on bows that are embroidered around them as well as all outlines and features. Home crafted from purchased kit. ca. 1940's (Courtesy Mrs. Frank Miller)

16″ "Betsy McCall" made with flesh color cotton broadcloth and cotton stuffing, yarn hair and embroidered features. Came with patterns for four dresses, jumper, jacket and undies. 1956.

6″ "Thumbsy," a 1962 doll from the Fuller Brush Co. All lithographed cloth with removable jacket, pants and scarf. Hat is glued on. Tag on body included: MADE FOR FULLER BRUSH CO. There is a very delightful Christmas poem about "Thumbsy" on the original box. Gift from good friend.

Shows 20″ "Wednesday" (M), 45″ "Morticia," Wednesday's mother (N), and 20″ "Pugsley" (P). 1962. Charles Addam's dolls from his cartoons. Designed by Paula Buxton for Aboriginals, Ltd.

15″ "Kuddles." All cloth with yellow yarn hair and original clothes. Marks: KNICKERBOCKER TOY CO., INC. 1965. (Courtesy Wendi Miller)

25″ "Dick Van Dyke" 1968 from movie "Chitty, Chitty, Bang, Bang." All cloth, pull string talker. Printed features, removable jacket and tie. Tag: MATTEL MR. POTTS. 1968 GLIDROSE PRODUCTS LTS. WARFIELD PRODUCTIONS LTD. 1968 MATTEL INC. HAWTHRONE, CALIF. (Courtesy Jeannie Mauldin)

16″ Robin Williams as "Mork." Pull string talker with ring on left side. All cloth that is printed and has tag on back of right leg: MATTEL COPYRIGHT 1979/PARAMOUNT PICTURES CORP. MATTEL INC. (Courtesy Shirley Pascuzzi)

16″ "W.C. Fields." Pull string talker. 1972. Tag: MADE BY KNICKERBOCKER TOY CO./DOLLS OF DISTINCTION on sewn in tag. All printed cloth. (Courtesy Jeannie Mauldin)

18″ "Betty Boop." All cloth with sewn on earrings, removable panties and dress. Tag: COPYRIGHT KING FEATURES SYNDICATE,INC. MADE BY COLOR-FORMS, INC. 1977. (Courtesy Treasure Trove)

16″ "Annie." All cloth dress is removable (with extreme patience). Painted features and tightly curled yarn hair. Tiny plush dog in pocket that is a body and head only and sewn in. Felt features. Tag: ANNIE/COPYRIGHT THE CHICAGO TRIBUNE 1977. Other side: KNICKERBOCKER TOY COMPANY.

16″ "Friendly Feeling." All cloth with printed features, and made in one piece. No question that he looks like Jimmy Carter although the name does not appear any place on tag. 1979.

14″ Talking "Dracula." All stuffed cloth with painted features, plush hair. Has pull string. Says things like: "The Drac is back," "I like to drive you battie." Tag: COMMONWEALTH TOY AND NOVELTY CO., INC. DESIGNED BY ROBIN KRAUSE. The box is made like a coffin, and he has a removable cape with his name on it.

Left: "Fairy Princess"; center: "Snow White"; right: "Little Red Riding Hood." All cloth dolls. Each doll has three aprons that open like a book with respective stories printed on the aprons. Tag: COPYRIGHT EMSON. REG. NO. OHIO 588 RECT. NO. PA. 347. MADE IN TAIWAN. (Courtesy Penny Pendlebury)

24″ Nursing African all cloth dolls. Yarn hair, felt features. Nursing twins snap on. Made by Bernita Maher from a pattern in 1980. (Courtesy Diane Hoffman)

11½″ "Pinocchio." All printed cloth. "Clothes" have printed poems and each fold up to make another character in the story. First is Pinocchio, second is Gepetto, third is Fairy, fourth is Cricket and fifth is real boy, First and last "head" is shown.

12″ "Cinderella"-Story Dress Doll. All stuffed cloth. Flesh color head, arms and upper torso. Lower torso is blue with sewn-on ruffle of lace, legs are white and shoes are blue. Painted blue eyes, yellow yarn hair. Gown has pictures and story around skirt. Doll is unmarked. Dress tag: DOLLS OF DISTINCTION/KNICKERBOCKER TOY CO. 1979.

12″ "Red Riding Hood." Same description as Cinderella-Story Dress Doll. Hood is sewn on. Removable cape. Eyes are painted brown and hair is in braids. Tag: DOLLS OF DISTINCTION/KNICKERBOCKER TOY CO. 1979.

19″ "Raggedy Ann" and "Andy" by Knickerbocker. All cloth with yarn hair. Each is designed to teach a child to zip, button, tie and snap. (Courtesy Amy Merrill)

Shown are four Lenci dolls with the "surprise" face. The two on the right have glass, flirting eyes which roll from side to side; the two on the left have painted eyes. Left front blonde is in white with red dots and trim. Left rear blonde is in a green, black and yellow provincial costume. Right front is in layers of pink and green and she has red hair. Right rear is all white with fur trim and she has black hair. All date from 1930's and have organdy gown with some having touchs of felt. All courtesy of Beppe Garella-Lenci, owner whose father owned the Lenci company for a great many years before him (mid-1930's). Standing behind the dolls is Mr. Beppe Garella-Lenci and the author.

## HISTORY OF LENCI

### Beginnings:

The company that eventually would bear the world famous LENCI name was begun in Turin, Italy in 1919 as a craft industry. Dolls were designed by well known Italian artists and crafted in pressed felt, a material indigenous to Turin. Wonderfully expressive and lifelike faces were painted on the shaped heads of the dolls, and finally they were dressed in clothes reflecting the styles of the period.

The trademark registered was "Ludus Est Nobis Constanter Industria," (To Play Is Our Constant Work) and was written in a circle around a child's spinning top, with the first letter of each word capitalized.

### Development:

By 1922, the dolls produced by the LENCI factory had achieved worldwide recognition, and were especially sought after in the United States. It was at this time that the initials of the Latin motto were first used to create the "LENCI" name.

During the 1920's, dolls available on the market had either flat rag heads which could not recreate the beauty of the human face, or had heads of porcelain which were too fragile for a child's play. The patented LENCI process, however, produced dolls using a material that was both beautiful and unbreakable.

The advent of depression and then war brought this success to a close. The LENCI factory diversified and continued to supply the Italian market with plush, Italian historical dolls, ceramic figurines and other items.

### Revival of the Classic Dolls:

Original LENCI dolls from the 1920's have become highly sought after collector's items, but good examples are scarce. The original moulds, catalogs, original models, the colors and the patterns for the doll's clothes all were preserved, however. Thus, influenced by a glorious tradition and stimulated by a remarkable increase in demand, LENCI has revived the production of these world famous dolls using the original equipment and methods from the 1920's.

Today, as in the 1920's, there is no doll the world over that can match the superb coloring, the beauty of expression, and the magnificent costuming of the LENCI.

27″ Lenci with the "Lillian Gish" face. Boudoir doll in original organdy dress with two tiered full skirt, edged in turquoise and green scalloped felt. Royal blue felt horizontal bands and 14 pink two-tone flowers and shaded green leaves sewn on. Royal blue felt bonnet with pink felt lining and plume feather. Fine white cotton half slip and pantaloons edged with organdy ruffles. High heels of royal blue suede with leather soles, silk stockings, garters with felt flowers in shades of yellow and green. Cotton tag on dress: LENCI/MADE IN ITALY. (Courtesy Glorya Woods)

16″ Early Lenci with "pouty" features, glued-on wig. All original clothes include a white short sleeve dress with black trim, blue coat and matching hat with black and white trim. Has embroidered tag attached to coat: LENCI/MADE IN ITALY. The back of the hat has a black tassel with a blue/black/white ball formed on the end.

Very large, over 36″, Oriental Lenci that is in a sitting position. The clothes are unbelivably beautiful, as are the detail of face and hair. She wears a very large gold decorative comb in back of hairdo. ca. 1924-1926. (Courtesy Mr. Beppe Garella-Lenci, owner of the Lenci firm)

An older Lenci (1920's). Very unusual face with rather downcast eyes that are painted. All original in brown, orange and yellow with black head, shawl with yellow/orange/white trim. Holds basket of felt tangerines. All clothes and doll are felt. (Courtesy Beppe Garella)

The Lenci dolls shown from this point on were re-introduced from 1978 through 1983 and are authentic Lenci dolls using mostly original designs and molds. World-wide production was strictly limited to 999 each. They are numbered on the backs of the heads and came with signed and numbered certificates of authenticity. They were produced in Turin (Italy) and are genuine LENCI dolls. Each doll comes in a dark blue box that opens in the middle. (New Lenci photos courtesy Tide-Rider, Inc.)

Lenci introduced 20″ "Susanna" of 1978 in basic white with three tones of blue trim and deep blue shoes and cap. Right is 20″ "Clo-Clo" in green with orange and green check, orange bodice, underside of hat with yellow rose. This doll was also made in a combination of deep blue and pinks.

27″ "Melania" of 1978 dressed in deep grey with pink flowers on skirt, pink hemline has deep grey trim. Deep grey shoes with pink trim. Sash is pink and gathered material ruffles the lower sleeves. Pink bonnet has cloth trim. Doll holds hankie. Light brown wig. On the right is 27″ "Rossella" in green/yellow and black plaid, yellow "blouse" and slip have black trim. Holds black purse with green trim and red and yellow rose buds. Large black and yellow hat with flowers around top.

Left: 20″ "Metelda" dressed in deep red and yellow, red shoes and matching red and yellow hat. Has two piece outfit with dress and coat with yellow buttons. Right: 27″ "Samantha" in royal blue with yellow trim and large matching hat. Wearing a blonde wig, she carries a pink rose. The blouse is pale blue material. Both are from 1979.

In 1979 Lenci also produced 20″ "Corinne," shown on the left, dressed in a two piece dress and jacket of orange and black with matching beanie style hat, black shoes and very dark wig. Right is 20″ "Colette" dressed in two tones of blue with blue shoes and matching hat. She has a medium blonde wig. Carries green, yellow and blue flowers. Blue satin bow at neck.

1980 introduced 20″ "Liviana" in a beige dress with blue trim on fluted hemline and white material slip showing. Blue shoes, blue/pink and red flowers on skirt. Blue bodice with pink sleeve cuffs, blue bonnet with pink ties. She has medium blonde wig. Right is 20″ "Vanessa" dressed in red and white check, white material pantaloons and red shoes. Her hat is red with green/red flowers and she holds a large pink and red rose. Black wig.

1980 saw the Lenci introduction of 20″ "Debora" on the left dressed in yellow and blue with yellow, black and green flowers attached to skirt and matching bonnet. Hem line has blue, yellow and black bands and shoes are black. Dark wig. Right is 20″ "Stefania" with blond wig. Wears a long pale green gown with deep green leaves and pink/red roses on skirt and on deep green bonnet, and black shoes.

During 1981 Lenci produced a boy "Mario" that is 20″, dressed in orange/pink trimmed short black pants, white material shirt and black jacket. The bow tie is orange and he has a matching cap, very dark wig, and black tie shoes. Right is 20″ "Patrizia" in pink gown with skirt with red bodice, pink material sleeves, red trim and has pink and red flowers on skirt. Matching pink and red bonnet with pale pink material tie, white material pantaloons with red shoes.

Lenci also made 27″ "Cristina" in 1981 with off-white gown with check pattern of deep purple/green, yellow/green trim, deep puple hem edging with green trim, matching bodice and hat. The sleeves match the skirt and she wears deep purple gloves with green cuffs. Right is 20″ "Violetta" in a combination of lavender and white with wide lace on bodice and lower sleeves. Lavender hat and shoes.

During 1982 Lenci introduced 20″ "Amanda" dressed in a gown of two tones of blue with deep navy squares on skirt and sleeves, blue shoes and bonnet. Right: 27″ "Fedora" in black with blue trim at hem and red trim at neck, ruffled white material lower sleeves with red trim and matching apron. The large hat is blue with red top side and she has red check and blue check flowers with two tone green leaves on skirt.

In 1982 Lenci also produced 20″ "Brunilde" in red dress and shoes with white dots, pockets, collar and sleeve cuffs. She has dark wig with red bows. Right is 20″ "Belinda" in green with white diamond patches, white bodice, green cap and shoes. There is dark green trim on shoes, button on cap, and around collar and bodice.

1982 saw four other models from the Lenci Company. Left to right: 16″ "Giovanna" in light and dark green, dark green shoes and hat, with white pinafore-style apron, with dark green felt trim. She has yellow and red flowers on hat and at waist. 16″ "Elisabetta" in all pink gown and hat with white dots and trim. Sitting is 16″ "Grazia" in pale blue trimmed in dark blue with large pink and red rose on drop waist dress. 16″ "Ellena" in three colors of pink with white band at waist and sleeve edge.

The 1983 series of Lenci dolls. Top row-left to right: "Bubi" in pale blue and white, a blue-eyed blonde haired boy. "Nanni" in beige overcoat, brown eyes and hair. "Antonia" in purple and pink with white, brown eyes and hair. Middle row: "Pluci the golfer", brown eyes and hair. "Claretta" in all red and white, dark hair & eyes. "Piera" in lavender and white with blue eyes and brown hair. "Suzanne the tennis player" in white, green and beige, blue eyes and brown hair. Front: "Mary" in green and red with brown eyes and brown hair, and "Lucy" in pale blue with red/white trim, blue eyes and brown hair. All are limited to 999 worldwide.

Mrs. Anili is a relative of the Lenci family, but it is known that the Lenci firm has published a statement in America concerning legal action in that the Lenci Company, "has summoned for judgement in the presence of the court of Torino, the firm Anili de Scavini Anili, demanding its condemnation for trademark infringement and acts of unfair competition due to advertising inserts and reports in...doll collector magazines." The Lenci statement also says, "The Lenci Company asserts that any dolls which in any way resemble Lenci, but are not marked Lenci, are only an imitation of models that are the exclusive property of the Lenci Company."

17″ "Certemonia" made by Anili. Signed with name on sole of foot. Dressed in pink felt and white organdy. Shows in detail the way the eyes of the Anili dolls are painted with much highlighting in the pupil and the long painted lashes. (Courtesy Glorya Woods)

Two dolls produced by Anili of Italy. The girl is 17″ "Bienchina" and is signed "Anili" on the left sole of foot. Pressed felt face mask, felt arms and legs with cotton bodies. Head turns. Dressed in pink organdy ruffled dress with felt flower trim, slip attached to dress and pink organdy ruffled panties. White cotton socks, pink felt shoes and felt flower in hair. The boy is 17″ "Pastorello" in pink felt jacket with felt flower trim, blue felt pants and hat with flower trim, white organdy shirt with lace trim, yellow felt sandals. He holds felt flowers. Has gold paper tag in back of outfit with flowers and the word: "Anili." (Courtesy Glorya Woods)

12″ Left: "Giada" and right: "Celestina" are felt with cloth bodies. Left: Pink and white organdy gown with deep rose jacket of felt with white buttons. Rose and white bonnet with white tie of satin. Rose, orange and blue flowers on skirt and hat. Right: Organdy gown of white with pale pink dots on skirt, bodice and brim of bonnet. White and rose flowers at waist. (Courtesy Glorya Woods)

8″ "Ginger" made by Cosmopolitan Doll Co. All hard plastic walker with sleep eyes, dressed in her original majorette outfit of white with gold trim, boots and hat with red feather. (Courtesy Pat Timmons)

8″ "Ginger" in original box. All hard plastic. These dolls could be purchased dressed in various outfits, or like this one, in just panties. Extra outfits were also sold separately. (Courtesy Pat Timmons)

11½″ "Flower Princess-LeeAnna." Excellent quality with plastic body, jointed waist, vinyl legs wit bendable knees, vinyl arms and head with rooted blonde hair. Green painted eyes, yellow gown with lavender/green/rose trim and flowers on ribbon around head. Marks: CREATA 1982, on head and lower back. Box: CREATA INTERNATIONAL, INC. 1982/MANHATTAN BEACH, CAL. 90266 (Courtesy Marie Ernst)

11½″ "Flower Princess-Laurelle" with same description as the "LeeAnna," but has open/closed smile mouth, blue painted eyes, pink gown with flowers at waist and in hair and pink frost in hair. (Courtesy Marie Ernst)

11½" "Flower Princess-Lisette" with exact same description as "LeeAnna." Dressed in lavender gown, has lavender hair and lavender eyes. Purple/lavender/pink trim and flowers. (Courtesy Marie Ernst)

8" "Pinocchio." This small doll is made of composition and jointed only at the shoulders. Painted features and hair, cloth clothes and felt hat. Shoes are modeled onto the doll. Marks: WALT DISNEY PROD./MADE IN USA/CROWN TOY CO. (Courtesy Diane Hoffman)

17" "Mary Poppins." Black cloth legs like hose, blue and white stripe body like gown and flesh color cloth arms. Head is vinyl with rooted hair, painted large blue eyes to side. Original blue and white stripe gown and white pinafore Has WALT DISNEY'S MARY POPPINS, on pinafore and gown is tagged: WALT DISNEY CHARACTER/COPYRIGHT WALT DISNEY PROD./J. SWEDIN. INC. LICENSEE. 1965. (Courtesy Kathy Feagans)

12" "Pluto." All plush with vinyl face mask. Felt fingers. Tag: PLUTO/WALT DISNEY PRODUCTION. Other side: WOOLY INC./360 SUYDAM ST/BROOKLYN 36, N.Y./MADE IN JAPAN.

11½″ "Small World" Dolls made for Disney World and Disneyland. All vinyl with joints at neck, shoulders and hips. Painted features and rooted hair. Marked: W. DISNEY PRODUCTIONS. They are miniatures of the automated figures that appear throughout the "Small World" ride at the Disney Parks. These dolls also come in a smaller size.

16″ "Goofy" All plush with felt features and a removable shirt. No marks.

13″ "Donald Duck." All plush with non-removable clothes. The eyes are plastic. Tag: KNICKERBOCKER, on one side and COPYRIGHT DISNEY PRODUCTIONS, on the other.

11½″ "Alice in Wonderland." Plastic and vinyl with painted eyes and marked: 2903/T/HORSMAN DOLLS, INC./1969, on head, HORSMAN DOLLS INC./T-11, on back. Doll is designed by Irene Szor. Green/white check dress with attached apron. Green and red trim. (Courtesy Treasure Trove)

11½″ "Cinderella." Plastic and vinyl with painted eyes, rooted blonde hair and dressed in one piece dress/pinafore that buttons in back, long white hose and has black ankle high boots. Marks: 8/HORSMAN DOLLS INC./1969. Has castle printed on pinafore. (Courtesy Treasure Trove)

8″ tall (doll and horse) "Fantasy Ride." Fairy Lady and Unicorn designed and made by Cheryl A. Vilbert, 1982. Every detail is extremely delicate and beautifully modeled.

30″ "Cathy." Made of papier mache with human hair wig. The body is jointed and there is an extra joint between the shoulder and elbow that lets the arm rotate. Made by an elderly lady who lives in Adelaide, South Australia. Only 20 made and 16 are owned by Beres Lindus of South Australia. Made in the 1940's.

30″ "Janet." 1940's. Made by lady in Adelaide, South Australia. Papier mache with human hair wig, has extra joint between shoulders and elbow so arm will rotate. (Courtesy Beres Lindus, South Australia)

16″ "Catherine de Medici" by Kathy Redmond. The shoulder plate, collar and snood in hair are gold fired porcelain. Dressed by Kathy Redmond.

18″ "Court Jester" made by Tita Varner. Has cloth body with porcelain head, arms and legs. Limited Edition of 25. 1981. Dressed by creator in beige, brown and gold with pale blue and beige ribbon.

15″ "Christmas Clown" with flesh-colored porcelain head and painted clown face. Beautiful painted Christmas Holly leaves at the corners of the eyes, modeled eyelids, and painted green eyes. Made in 1979 by J. & L. Gabrielson.

24″ "Clown" with beautiful butterfly painted on face. Porcelain head, glass and glued-on wig. Designed and created by Florence Baker, who was the original artist to make dolls with painted butterflies in various colors. Many copies of this idea are now being made by others. 1980-1982.

14″ "Golden Anniversary," also called the lady of "Two Fans" made by NIADA Doll Artist, Halle Blakley. Sculptured cloth-like face with painted features and a cloth covered wire armature style body. Comes attached to wooden stand.

28″ Wax dolls made by Bramble & Pinager. The "white" one is the prototype of the ones in porcelain called "Sara." Both have glass eyes and the modeling is extremely fine, delicate and very beautiful. (Courtesy Barbara Earnshaw)

9″ Designed by artist Jerry Kott. Hand painted wood head, stuffed velvet body with satin over wood arms. Hand signed on leg: 1976 KOTT/ BOLESTRIDGE. Sold for $45.00 in fine stores. (Courtesy Marge Meisinger)

A fantastic artist in wood is Robert Smith, who designs and carves, then finely polishes life size wood dolls. This one is "Floozie." He discovers personalities as the wood is worked down to fine detail. (Courtesy Robert Smith)

7½″ tall "Shirley Temple" made by Virginia M. Downing. 1981. Made of sculpture compound and painted with oils. The Shirley has 56 curls and is dressed in pink, from the movie "Curly Top."

9″ "PIDD." The all needlepoint doll made by A.P. Miller of Houston Texas. She is made in 10 pieces, head and body front and back, front and back arms and legs and hair is same yarn as used for needlepoint. (Courtesy A.P. Miller collection)

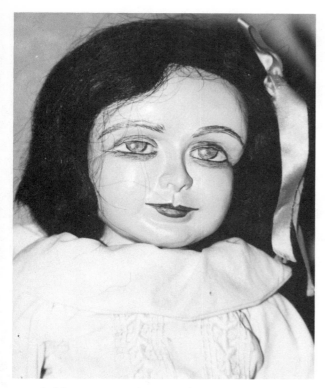

20″ Child Joan Crawford made by R. Lane Herron, and once owned by Joan Crawford. (Courtesy Kimport Dolls)

A "Pennydoll" Original of Helen Hunt Jackson's fictional character "Romona." The artist and owner is Penny Pendlebury and a member of ODCACA Doll Artists Association. (Courtesy Penny Pendlebury)

These all cloth dolls are "The Photographer and His Wife" created as a cartoon series, made and designed by Phyllis Teague. The dolls are patterned after Phyllis's brother, Doug, and wife, Lois. (Courtesy Phyllis Teague)

14″ "Courtney" that is made of brushed felt and jointed at neck, shoulders and hips. Designed and made by Debbie Anderson. (Courtesy June Schultz)

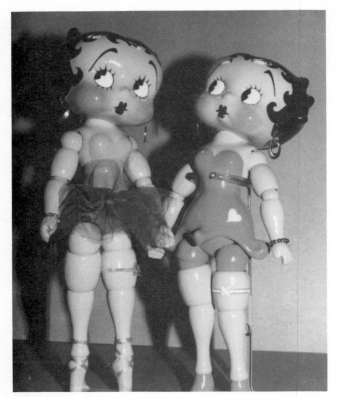

12″ "Betty Boop." Composition, fully jointed as were the original ones. The Ballerina is in pink with painted pink body suit, pink material tu tu, ballet slippers, garter, bracelets and gold loop earrings. The other has painted blue clothes, shoes and garter. Marked: RICHARD GAYNOR AND LYNN MOTTER 1982. (Courtesy Glorya Woods)

Limited Edition 12″ "Kewpie" with brown glass eyes, jointed composition body and marked: 1980 ALICE HOOVER #9. Shows another view of the mother and baby. (Courtesy Glorya Woods)

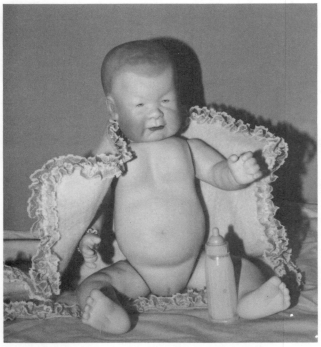

20″ "Someone Special." All bisque and fully jointed. Life size infant and a Limited Edition of 50 boys and 50 girls. 1981. The exclusive copyright design is by Keepsake Original Dolls. (Courtesy Phyllis Teague)

18″ "Tiny Tots" made by doll artist Christine Adams. All hand made. They look very much like the early Kathe Kruse dolls of Germany. Cloth bodies and limbs with stitched fingers. 1981-1982 (Courtesy Kimport Dolls)

"Morning Star" created by Mountain Babies Dolls 1982. She was made after much study and sculpturing done while interviewing woodland Indians from the Columbia River area. The woodland Indians wore buckskin and the coastal Indians of Washington used chewed bark for clothing. Actual glass beads decorated "Morning Star's" costume and are sewn as they actually were long ago. The tiny cradleboard doll she holds is also very authentic. The doll has a human hair wig and glass eyes. The basic bone and body sculpture was developed from photos and observations of the three year old Indian child. (Courtesy Bessie Carson)

4' 7" tall "Gregory Lurie" wears boy's size 10-12 clothes. Sculptured after designer-makers son, Gregory. All cloth, stuffed with foam, with human hair wig, painted features and dressed in exact clothes that Gregory wore. Wynona Lurie has also dressed the doll in look-a-like outfits such as baseball uniforms and dress clothes. Made and owned by Wynona Lurie. 1978.

7″ "Bride" of Poland. All hard plastic with sleep eyes and painted lashes. One piece body and legs. No marks on doll. Tag: POLISH BRIDE.

7½″ "Duchess." All hard plastic. Painted on white shoes with bow. Sleep blue eyes/molded lashes and no painted lashes. Hair and all clothes are pink.

7″ "Groom." All hard plastic, jointed at neck and shoulders. Painted man's hairdo, sleep eyes. Clothes are stapled on, plus two thumb tacks in back and one in front to represent buttons. Molded-on black shoes (bows on toes). Marks: DUCHESS DOLL CORP/DESIGN COPYRIGHT 1948. (Courtesy Virginia Jones)

7″ "Roy Rogers" and "Dale Evans." He is jointed at the neck and shoulder, has blue sleep eyes, green chaps, green & white check shirt, yellow felt vest and holster with gold brads, red cuffs, hot pink scarf, white hat and a gold "buckle" on the belt. She has white blouse, vest and skirt, green cuffs, yellow holster and gold buckle. Also a yellow/green tie on white hat and a hot pink scarf. Both have painted-on shoes. (Courtesy Virginia Jones)

6″ "September Morn" designed by Grace Drayton. Made of chalk with molded blonde hair, painted eyes and "ooh" style mouth. (Courtesy Glorya Woods)

6″ "Felix the Cat." Marks: FELIX THE CAT. 1962. FELIX THE CAT PRODUCTIONS. EASTERN MOULDED PRODUCTIONS, on back. All vinyl. (Courtesy Shirley Pascuzzi)

# Eegee Doll Company

The name of this company is made up from the name of the owner and founder, E.G. Goldberger. The company was founded in 1917, and the early dolls are marked E.G., then later E.G. Goldberger and now EEGEE, although the name Goldberger will appear on tags and boxes.

In 1952 this company issued two sets of dolls, "Jack and Jill" and "Hansel and Gretel" which looked very much like the Gobel Hummel dolls of that period. They were vinyl with oversized white plastic shoes.

In November of 1955 the Eegee Company entered into a contract with Mollye Goldman to work for them (35 hours a week) as designer, pattern drafter, and advisor-supervisor of quality control. Mollye retained this position until the end of September, 1957. Beginning October 1, 1957, Mollye Goldman was retained by contract with Egee until December 31, 1957, with another contract found to be binding between November 1, 1956 until January 31, 1957. These two contracts bound Mollye Goldman to make doll clothes for the Eegee Company during these periods of time exclusively from her own factory in Drexill Hill, PA.

Some of the clothes designed and made by Mollye during her contract time with Eegee will be found in this Volume.

23″ "Susan Stroller." hard plastic body with jointed knees, vinyl head with rooted hair, sleep blue eyes and the limbs are strung. 1955. (Courtesy Phyllis Teague)

26" "Connie." Early stuffed vinyl with wire through legs so they were posable. Vinyl head with rooted hair and sleep eyes. Clothes designed by Mollye Goldman. Also came in 17" size. 1956.

15" "Angel Face" with rooted hair and sleep eyes and has one piece stuffed vinyl body with wire through legs so they are posable. Clothes designed by Mollye Goldman. 1956.

17" All early stuffed vinyl with wired legs that are posable. Vinyl head with sleep eyes, open/closed mouth and rooted hair. Made for Woolworths in 1956 by the Eegee Doll Company, with clothes designed by Mollye Goldman. Did not have a name.

22" "Cuddle Bun" with vinyl head and molded hair, sleep eyes. The molded hair is pulled up to the back and she has drop curls with deep modeling. The body is all stuffed vinyl with wired legs so she can sit. The dress was designed and made for Eegee by Mollye Goldman. 1956.

12″ "Bunting Baby" made for the Woolworth chain in 1955 and 1956. Doll has vinyl head, molded hair, sleep eyes and all vinyl stuffed body. Outfit designed and made by Mollye Goldman under contract to Eegee.

25½″ "Bunting Baby" made for Woolworth by Egee and with clothes designed by Mollye Goldman. Vinyl head with molded hair and sleep eyes. Body is all stuffed vinyl with 2nd and 3rd finger of left hand molded together and curled and 2nd and 3rd inger on right hand deeply curled into palm. Has two upper teeth inset. 1956.

20″ "Little Debutante." All vinyl with vinyl head, rooted hair and sleep eyes. Jointed shoulders and hips. High heel feet. Outfit designed by Mollye Goldman for Eegee. 1957.

17″ "Little Debutante." Clothes made and designed by Mollye Goldman. Also came in a 14½″-15″ size. Jointed at shoulders and hips. 1957.

18″ "Sue Ann." All vinyl with rooted hair and sleep eyes. Clothes made and designed by Mollye Goldman. 1958.

10½″ Version of "My Fair Lady" as shown in the Eegee catalog. Doll could be purchased in bra and girdle and had six separate packaged outfits. Vinyl head with rooted hair, sleep eyes, rigid vinyl body and limbs with jointed waist. High heel feet. Came as brunette and blonde. All the "My Fair Lady" clothes were designed by Mollye Goldman. 1957.

4″ "Eskimo" purchased in Canada in 1968. All vinyl with molded on panties, one piece body and limbs and original clothes. Marks: EEGEE CO. #36. (Courtesy Wendi Miller)

9½″ "Honey Lamb." Also there was "Calico Kitty." Has brown rooted hair and brown painted eyes. Plastic and vinyl. Painted eyes. Made by Eegee Co. 1978-1979.

17″ "Softina Toddles." Brown rooted hair, sleep brown eyes and one piece body and limbs. Jointed at neck only. Original clothes. Marks: EEGEE CO./17ST, on head; EEGEE CO./15WN, 1979, on body. (Courtesy Mrs. Frank Miller)

20″ "Baby Boo Hoo." Vinyl arms, legs, and head with foam filled cloth body that zips open for battery case and record. She cries when pacifier is removed. Original clothes. Marks: GOLDBERGER DOLL MFG. CO., INC./BROOKLYN NEW YORK, 11237, on tag. (Courtesy Wendi Miller)

10″ "Daydreams—Sweet Things." All vinyl with rooted hair, large vivid blue sleep eyes. Open mouth/nurser and all original. (Courtesy Phyllis Teague)

12″ "Dolly Parton." Plastic with vinyl head and limbs. Bendable knees, jointed waist. Has additional outfits. Painted features. Marks: DOLLY PARTON/EEGEE CO/HONG KONG, on head and back. Box: GOLDBERGER MFG. CO. 1980.

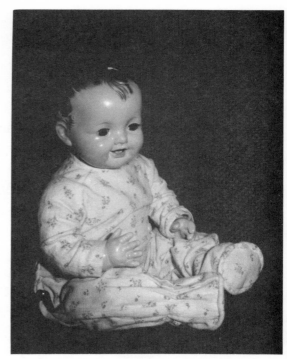

16″ "Cunning Baby." 1918-1920. All composition and has jointed wrists with hard rubber hands, gray celluloid over tin sleep eyes. Replaced wig. Marked: EFFANBEE, in script, on back. (Courtesy Shirley Merrill)

18″ Marked: EFFANBEE/LOVUMUS/PAT. 1,283,558. All composition with bent baby legs, molded hair, sleep eyes and open mouth with two upper and lower teeth. Date unknown. (Courtesy Joleen Flack)

24″ Marked: EFFANBEE, on back of the shoulder. Composition shoulder head and limbs with stuffed cloth body, grey tin sleep eyes and glued-on human hair brown wig. (Courtesy Edith Evans)

24″ "Rosemary." Composition shoulder plate head and limbs with cloth body. Tin sleep eyes, open mouth with four teeth and has human hair wig. Marks: EFFANBEE/ROSEMARY/WALK-TALK-SLEEP. 1925. (Courtesy Glorya Woods)

22″ "Patsy Lou." All composition with left arm bent at elbow, molded hair and sleep eyes. Marks: PATSY LOU/EFFANBEE, on back. 1930's. (Courtesy Joleen Flack)

22″ "Patsy Lou" with wig over molded hair. All composition, sleep eyes and left arm bent at elbow. Marks: PATSY LOU/EFFANBEE, on back. 1929-1930's. (Courtesy Joleen Flack)

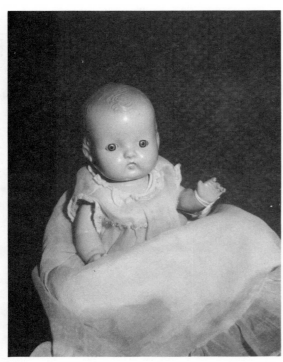

10″ "Patsy Baby" of 1932. All composition with lightly molded hair, sleep celluloid over tin eyes and closed mouth. Marks: EFFANBEE/PATSY BABY. (Courtesy Joleen Flack)

14″ "Patricia." All composition with brown sleep eyes, brown human hair wig and original clothes. Marks: EFFANBEE PATRICIA, on back. 1932. (Courtesy Shirley Merrill)

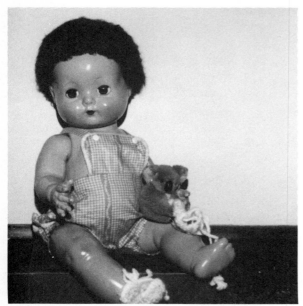

16″ 1930's "Sweetie Pie," "Mickey" or "Baby Bright Eyes." All composition with strung arms, legs and head. Lambs wool wig, sleep brown eyes, closed tiny mouth, dimples under eyes. Open hands and fat legs. Marks: EFFANBEE, on back and head. (Courtesy Jeannie Mauldin)

10″ "Patsy Baby." Composition head with molded, painted hair, brown tin sleep eyes, jointed cloth body and limbs. Celluloid hands. All original. White dimity undies and dress with pink braid trim, pink silk crepe short coat with matching bonnet, tatted lace trim. The legs are long and the *ICE SKATES ARE ORIGINAL.* Purchased as shown in a Denver Dry Goods store in the early 1930's. The regular Patsy Babies in this outfit have long coats and dresses. (Courtesy Carolyn Altfather)

24″ tall Deweese Cochran designed mannequin named "Cindy." Composition-like material with painted eyes and human hair wig. The arms are detachable, otherwise she is made all in one piece. Painted on shoes and socks. The wooden stand advertising "Honeysuckle" childrens' clothes is made in two pieces. (Courtesy Sheryl Schmidt)

27″ "Little Lady." All composition with rubber latex arms with paint overlay. Wide set fingers that will take gloves. Sleep blue eyes and yarn hair. The yarn wigged dolls mostly came with painted eyes. ca. 1942-1945. She has been re-dressed. (Courtesy Sheryl Schmidt)

The 1938 Ward's catalog shows the Deweese Cochran doll on the left called "America's Child," and also the "Anne Shirley" doll with coronet braids wrapped around the head. "Anne Shirley" was available in sizes 15″, 17½″ and 21″. At right is the 15″ "Anne Shirley" with human hair braids wrapped around head. Mint, all original clothes. Dress is cotton plaid of rose, blue and yellow with satin Effanbee tag. Organdy pinafore with eyelet trim, pink imitation leather shoes, rayon socks, also came with natural straw sailor style hat with rose color grosgrain ribbon. Childhood doll of Betty Selby, whose twin sister had same doll with blonde braided wig, cotton plaid dress in blue, rose and yellow, blue imitation leather shoes and hat with blue grosgrain ribbon. Marks: ANNE SHIRLEY/EFFANBEE, on back. (Courtesy Glorya Woods)

17″ "Little Lady." Painted eyes, body of pink cloth, made in the 1940's when materials were scarce. Gauntlet composition hands, composition head. Replaced wig and clothes. Many of these dolls made during World War II had yarn hair. (Courtesy Lilah Beck)

13″ "Candy Kid." All jointed composition, blue sleep eyes, molded hair and all original as shown in 1946 Wards catalog. Replaced shoes. (Courtesy Shirley Merrill)

20″ "Black Little Boy." All hard plastic with glued-on caracul wig, sleep eyes, original boy's outfit. This was a trial doll made in 1951, and only very few were purchased by retailers. Marked: EFFANBEE, on head and back.

21″ "Rootie Kazootie" and "Polka Dottie" with vinyl head and limbs with vinyl coated bodies. Modeled hair, large painted eyes, both have wide open/closed mouths. These dolls also came in an 11″ size with vinyl heads but on latex bodies. He is dressed in blue romper suit and she in white with red, yellow and blue polka dots. 1953. (Courtesy Jeannie Mauldin)

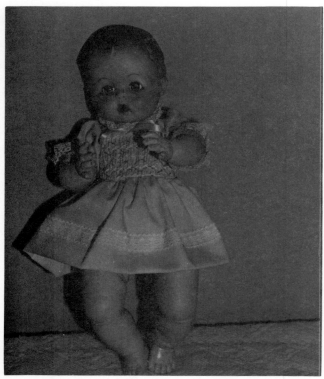

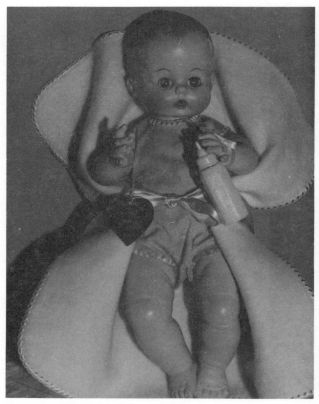

16″ "Twinkie" of 1959. All heavy vinyl with molded hair, sleep eyes, open mouth/nurser and dressed in pink with white and blue trim. (Courtesy Jeannie Mauldin)

16″ 1980 "Twinkie" has a lighter color vinyl and it is also a thinner vinyl than the 1959 version. Molded hair, sleep eyes, open mouth/nurser and dressed in pink romper suit, tied with pink sash on white fleece blanket with pink trim. (Courtesy Jeannie Mauldin)

15″ "Patsy Ann." Jointed rigid vinyl with vinyl head, rooted hair, sleep blue eyes and freckles. Marks: EFFANBEE PATSY ANN/1959, on head. All original in sailor style dress of red and white with blue trim on collar. (Courtesy June Schultz)

20" and 7½" Mother and child. Baby is all vinyl with molded hair, open/closed mouth and dressed in white fleece snow suit. Has fully jointed body. Mother has an all hard plastic body, vinyl head with rooted saran hair, blue sleep eyes and marked: EFFANBEE, on head. She also has jointed knees. Dressed in blue coat, pill box hat, both trimmed with lace. White dress with blue apple print. White gloves, earrings, wedding ring set, metal heart wrist tag. 1957. (Courtesy Ann Wencel)

30" "Mary Jane." All vinyl, flirty eyes. Walks. Marks: EFFANBEE MARY JANE 1960, on head. Shown with Steiff dog, "Snobby." (Courtesy June Schultz)

"Most Happy Family." Mother is 18" with hard plastic body and limbs and vinyl head, rooted hair and sleep eyes. Dressed in blue silk, brown straw pill box hat, pearl drop earrings, wedding band and engagement ring. 9" Baby has painted eyes, heart rattle and in white bunting suit. 8½" Sister, "Fluffy," and 8" Brother, "Mickey," both in blue silk with boy having white shirt and black tie. ca. 1962. (Courtesy Betty Cossiboin)

10" Effanbee marked: EFFANBEE/LITTLE LADY/FLUFFY, on head. Very soft vinyl head with rooted hair and inset brown eyes. Regular vinyl body jointed at neck, shoulders and hips. Not original clothes. (Courtesy Virginia Dean)

18" "Suzie Sunshine" that is Black and has black freckles. Plastic with vinyl head and arms. Not original clothes. Rooted black hair. Marks: EFFANBEE/1961. (Courtesy Virginia Dean)

11" "Holly." A 1983 limited doll made for a select number of stores with only 1500 made. Each comes with a letter and signed Certificate of Identity and signed by the President of Effanbee Doll Corp., Roy Raizen. Letter is also signed by LeRoy Fadem, Chairman of the Board of Effanbee. Dressed in red and white with green applied holly leaves on hat and skirt. Marks on doll are: EFFANBEE/1975/1976. Gift from a very special friend.

The Effanbee Doll Company has made a number of special order dolls. Following is a partial list.

13" "Yellow Rose of Texas" for Sanger-Harris of Dallas, 1981. Dressed in long yellow gown with two large ruffles at hem, a large yellow picture hat and has lace trim over shoulders and edging of hat. Has bouquet of yellow roses tied to one hand.

13" "Lady With A Velvet Hat" for the Smithsonian Institution, 1981. Dressed in gown of maroon taffeta with white collar that is layered and stands up around the face. White feather hat and buckled belt.

11" "Miss Amanda" for Amway Products, 1981-1982. Her gown has a peach skirt, cream color bodice and sleeves with peach yoke, wide lace at hem and detachable lace collar shawl style. Feather on peach color ribbon tied in hair.

19" Special "Just for Kids" Floppy Doll for Winterbrook Corp., 1981. The cloth body and limbs are red and white check and the doll uses the "Susie Sunshine" head with blonde rooted hair. The dress is white with red and white sleeves, has a red and white check ruffle at hem. There is a half round pocket on front of the dress with a black and white Teddy bear printed on it. The shoes are black and have a white insert with two black buttons. This "Floppy" doll (not the outfit) was used in the Enchanted Garden series #2729-1982 and the 1981 Over The Rainbow series #2728.

11" Bea in Her Bonnet For the Bear Creek Co., of Medford, Oregon, 1981. This doll was similar to the Currier & Ives doll in multi-flowered gown with deep rose trim and lace, deep rose bonnet with large bow.

Carson Pirie Scott of Chicago, 1982, had a special doll made in red/white/blue to promote American-made merchandise. She has on long pantaloons, dress with stripe skirt, dark bodice with long sleeves, lace at neck and cuffs. White eyelet lace shoulder strap apron and a large bow in hair that matches the skirt.

Foley's of Houston, 1982, had a special doll called "Magnolia," 13" and dressed in pink and white candy striped gown with ruffle at hem, white bodice, straw hat with large pink bow.

Carson Pirie Scott of Chicago, 1983, had an 11" "Ballerina" in lavender tutu with white, and headpiece trimmed in rhinestones. She was called "The Sugar Plum Fairy."

Gimbels, 1983, had a limited edition of "Tara," a 16" doll dressed in a pink strapless taffeta gown with tulle overskirt and three tulle ruffles in the skirt, and a stole. Pink ribbon sash and bow in back of hair.

Meyer's of New Jersey, 1983, had an 11" limited edition 1914 "Dolly Shopper" to commemorate their 70th year in business. She is dressed "Gibson" style with navy full length skirt, white top with puffed long sleeves, white flat brim straw hat with navy band and red roses at sides. She also has rose and ribbon at neckline. Attached to arm is basket with a baby doll in it and the Meyer's sticker on the side.

Treasure Trove, Manhasset, New York, 1983, had a edition of 500 Black Brides, the only black 13" Effanbee doll. Named "Annabelle".

11″ "The Sugar Plum Fairy." A Limited Edition created for Carson Pirie Scott & Co. White leotards, white slippers with pink ribbon ties. Purple tutu with white trim and head piece trimmed in rhinestones. Pink ribbon around neck. Marks: EFFANBEE 1976/1/76 on head. EFFANBEE, on back. Plastic and vinyl with dark hair and sleep eyes. (Courtesy Marie Ernst)

11″ "Castle Garden" from the Currier and Ives Collection. Pale blue skirt and sleeves with deep purple bodice and wrap around overskirt. White hat with blue ribbon tie, purple bow and blue flowers. White shoes. 1979 and 1980 only.

Left: 11″ "A Night on the Hudson" from the Currier & Ives Collection. Blue satin gown with white trim, blue bonnet with white net tie and bow on top. 1978 only. Right: "Plymouth Landing" of same collection. Deep burgandy gown with burgandy trim. Lace in front with burgandy tie and cameo, matching bonnet with net tie and trim. 1979 and 1980 only. The 1979 doll has wider spaced trim at hem and a shorter lace "bib."

11″ Left: "Wayside Inn"; and right: "Life in the Country" from the Currier & Ives Collection. Both discontinued in 1980. Left: Blue ruffled gown with wide ruffled collar and sleeves. Royal blue bodice and waist wrap with wide ruffle trim. Matching bonnet. Blue in 1978 and 1980, but the 1970 version was in green. Right: Beige flowered gown with burgandy and lace trim, matching bonnet and cameo at neck.

15″ "Colonial Lady" from the Passing Parade Collection. Made in 1977 and 1978 only. Flowers printed on blue background with white trim overskirt, white cap, slip, pantaloons and pumps.

11″ "Central Park" of the Currier and Ives Collection is on the left with beige satin gown and waist wrap with two ruffles at hem, fringe trim at sleeves and lower edge of wrap plus green ribbon sash, matching bonnet has brown feather. Made in 1978 only. Right: 11″ "Charleston Harbor" from same collection. Pink gown and over skirt, matching bonnet with all having black trim. Some had beige or black feather trim on bonnet. Made in 1980 only.

Bridal Set of 1979 included 18″ "Bride" with the Nicole face. 15″ Bridesmaid with the Caroline face, "Ringbearer" and "Flowergirl" are Pun'kins. "Bridesmaids" are in white over blue slips and a blue bodice. "Ringbearer" has blue short pants outfit and white shirt with blue tie. The pillow is blue with white lace. Both the little ones have red rooted hair. (Courtesy Hazel Adams)

16″ "Anchors Aweigh" boy and girl in white with navy trim and red ribbon ties. Designed by Faith Wick. 1979 and 1980. (Courtesy Hazel Adams)

11″ Black version of "Summer" of the Four Seasons Series. Purchased in 1980. Marks: EFFANBEE/ 1976/1176, on head; EEF & BEE on back. All white organdy gown trimmed with lace and pink satin ribbon sash, roses on hat and in basket tied to wrist. First made in 1976, but clothes remained the same to 1980. (Courtesy Hazel Adams)

11″ "Babette" of the Petite Filles Collection, which also included 16″ size dolls. Dressed in antique color satin with floral print with straw hat and pink ribbon. 1980 only. (Courtesy Hazel Adams)

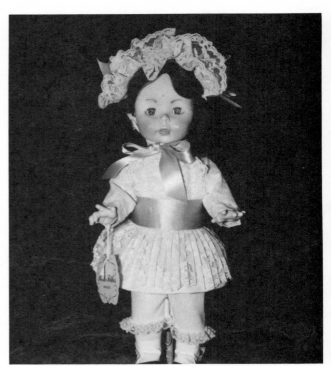

16″ "Monique" of the Petite Filles Collection. In antique color satin and lace and blue ribbon sash and on hat as well as tie. Black shoes with white side button spats. 1980. (Courtesy Hazel Adams)

11″ "Mimi" from the Petite Filles Collection. 1980. Marks: EFFANBEE/1966, on head. White lace & organdy over blue with matching bonnet. Black slippers and white spats that snap to the sides. 1980.

11″ "Saratoga" of the Grand Dames Collection. Came in White only, but 125 of a Limited Edition were made for Treasure Trove in 1981. Gown and hat are black and white. (Courtesy Hazel Adams)

17″ "John Wayne" made in 1981 only. Part of the Legendary Series by Effanbee Doll Company. All vinyl and dressed in authentically designed outfit from his own wardrobe. Carries excellent quality scale rifle. (Courtesy Marilyn Hitchcock)

The 1982 "Just Friends" Collection was three pairs of girls and boys: On top are the "Alpine Hikers," left is "Swiss Yodeler" and right dolls are "Dutch Treat." The "Alpine Hikers" were made in 1982 only and replaced with "Fortune Cookie," a boy and girl of China dressed in red and black. The complete sets will be discontinued in 1984.

All the 1982 outfits for the "Bobbesy Twins" were discontinued in 1983. They came dressed in red plaid with extra outfits in boxes. *Out West* is navy and red, *Go A Sailing* is red/white and blue. *At The Seashore* is navy and white and *Winter Wonderland* is navy and red. The dolls continued with different outfits for 1983, and dolls are being discontinued in 1984. "The Bobbsey Twins" are from books written by Laura Lee Hope.

The 1982 "Absolutely Abigail" Collection: Left to right is the boy "Cousin Jeremy," behind him is "Recital Time" in peach and lace, front center is "Sunday Best" floral pink and lace, in back is "Strolling in the Park" and far right: "Afternoon Tea." The only doll from this series that was discontinued in 1983 was "Strolling in the Park." She was replaced with "Garden Party" dressed in light rose satin and lace. The entire set was discontinued in 1984.

John Wayne as "Guardian of the West" was made for the Legend Series in 1982. The Legend Dolls are made for one year only. This series began in 1981 with W.C. Fields, 1982 was an older looking John Wayne in cowboy clothes. 1982 also had Mae West (only year with two dolls in this series) and 1983 had Groucho Marx. The John Wayne of 1983 is 18″ tall and one third of the royalities paid for either Wayne doll went to the John Wayne Memorial Cancer Research Fund at U.C.L.A.

16″ "Sherlock Holmes" made by Effanbee for the Limited Edition Fan Club for 1983. Excellent modeling with extremely fine detailed molded brown hair and grey costume with shirt, black pants and high top shoes. Painted blue eyes and holds plastic curved pipe. (Author)

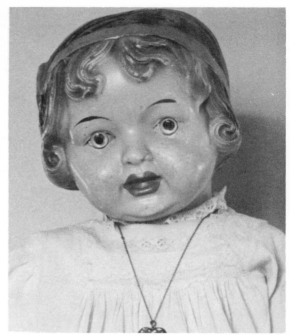

30″ Marked: ELECTRA TOY & NOVELTY CO. N.Y. Cloth body with ¾ composition arms, composition shoulder plate head with molded hair and painted blue eyes. Wears original clown suit. (Courtesy Kay Bransky)

34″ Marked: ELECTRA TOY & NOVELTY CO. N.Y. Cloth body that is excelsior filled, ¾ composition arms, shoulder plate head of composition with painted straw color hair and blue molded ribbon. Two wires out the neck when touched to a battery make the inset glass eyes light up. This doll is listed as being "Amy" of 1912. (Courtesy Kay Bransky)

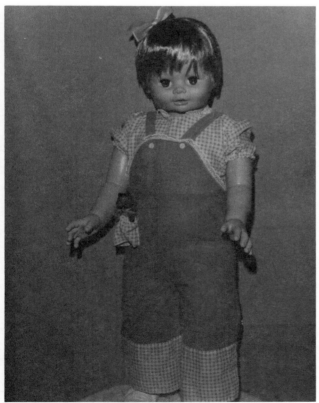

30″ "Baby Two Year Old." Vinyl head and arms with plastic body and legs. Sleep eyes, open/closed mouth and short rooted hair. Came in this original two piece outfit in either pink or blue. Marks: EUGENE DOLL 1978 53100. Has a little Teddy Bear attached near the hip. (Courtesy Phyllis Teague)

14½″ "Lil Gypsy." Rooted curly hair, painted features and freckles. Blue and white check dress, blue hat. Thumb on right hand sticks out, vinyl head and hands, stuffed cloth body and arms and legs. Tag on body: MADE IN TAIWAN R.O.C. Marked on head: 11/EUGENE DOLL CO./1978. (Courtesy Carol Friend)

7", 6", 5" and 4½" "Gnome Family." All plastic with vinyl arms and heads. All have sculptured hair except the girl, who has rooted yellow hair. All have swivel ball posable heads and are jointed at hips and shoulders. All have painted features. Hats are glued on. Marks: EUGENE DOLLS/MADE IN HONG KONG, on backs.

Shows the "Roberta"-"Sandra" doll from the 1946 Montgomery Ward catalog dressed in the same outfit as the doll shown below.

17" "Roberta" that is all composition with brown sleep eyes and a beautifully molded face. Her clothes are excellent quality and are tagged: MADE IN U.S.A./EUGENIA DOLL CO. NY 3 NY/AMERICA'S FINEST DOLLS. She is marked only with a 17 on her back. Box: A PERSONALITY/PLAMATE/STYLED FOR/MONTGOMERY WARDS/48D-56 BY EUGENIA DOLL CO. Her wrist tag says MY NAME IS ROBER-TA, but the Montgomery Ward catalog (1946) calls her Sandra. (Courtesy Jeannie Shipi)

12″ "Angel." All vinyl with molded hair, inset blue eyes, pug nose and well defined fingers and toes. Not original clothes. Marks: FIELD ENTERPRISES 1966. She was made by the M & S Doll Company and under that heading the reader will find same doll with clothes available for her. She was listed under Mfg. Unknown, page 226 of *Modern Collector Dolls, Vol. 1.* (Courtesy Shirley Pascuzzi)

14″ Made from "Baby Ann" by unknown company. Cloth body and legs as well as arms, vinyl hands. Vinyl head with rooted hair, painted black eyes, "shoes" are sewn on, as is the dress. Marks: unreadable except last word that is PRODUCT. Eyes are painted much larger with longer lashes than the "Baby Ann" by Fisher-Price.

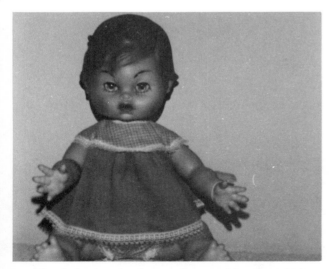

15″ Plastic body, vinyl arms, legs and head with deeply molded yellow hair, sleep blue eyes, open/closed mouth and open hands. Doll is extremely well modeled. Original clothes. Marks: INDUSTRIES BAR-TARLAS (ARGENTINA), in circle on head. (Courtesy Jeannie Mauldin)

15″ "Pebbles" with cloth body, vinyl head and limbs. Rooted bright red hair, large painted black eyes and in original clothes, which are black and green. Marks: 1980/HANNA BARBERA, INC./MIGHTY STAR/CANADA/H.B. 14. Has white plastic bone in hair.

These three scenes are from a large department store in Peking, China and shows the toy section. These photos were taken in 1979. The doll parts sell for 1.50 yuan which is 75 cents in U.S. currency. By the time the Chinese get a doll "built" it is not particularly cheap. (Photos courtesy Margaret Mandel)

6½″ Chinese children with bisque heads, hands and feet, stuffed cloth bodies and painted features. ca. 1910. Both original. (Courtesy Betty Wood)

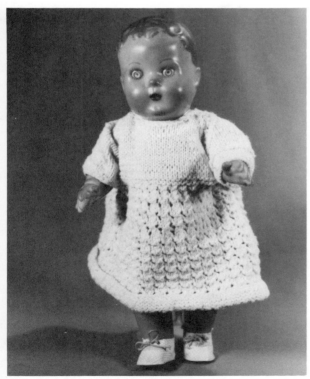

15″ "Marie Lou" made of Lastic Plastic in 1947. A toddler with inset celluloid covered eyes, closed mouth and molded hair, painted brown. Very yellow-orange, but not sticky as most early vinyls are. In old crocheted outfit. Marks: "MARY LOU"/ PRO. PAT. 30169-45/31719-47, LASTIC PLASTIC, on head; MORMIT PRODUCT/MADE IN ENGLAND, low on back. (Courtesy Jayn Allen)

8″ All hard plastic with sleep eyes and mohair wig. Original "Queen" outfit. Made by Rosebud of England. (Courtesy Marge Meisinger)

8″ All hard plastic with sleep eyes and mohair wig. Tag: VASTERGOTLAND J.W./JILL Marks: ROD-DY/MADE IN ENGLAND, on back. (Courtesy Marge Meisinger)

7½″ Boy and girl made in England. She has black lambs-wool wig and he has painted black hair. Both have molded on shoes with painted black soles, sleep eyes with molded lashes, painted lashes under eyes only. Clothes stapled on. (Courtesy Joan Amundsen)

7″ Older "Guardsman" by Peggy Nesbit. Made in England. Composition type material and bent arms. (Courtesy Renie Culp)

8″ Peggy Nesbit 1977 "King Arthur" and a Limited Edition of 350. Costumed of the 15th Century and cast of a special styrene composition with hand painted features. Original. Tag: COSTUME DOLL BY PEGGY NESBIT. (Courtesy Marilyn Hitchcock)

8″ Peggy Nesbit 1977 "Sir Lancelot," which was a Limited Edtion of 350. Costume of the 15th Century. Cast of special styrene composition with hand painted features. Original. Tag: COSTUME DOLLS BY PEGGY NESBIT. (Courtesy Marilyn Hitchcock)

14″ Oriental with yellow flesh tones, black rooted hair, painted black eyes and wears original clothes. Marks: CLODREY 7203/MADE IN FRANCE. (Courtesy Shirley Merrill)

14″ Sexed boy and girl. All vinyl, rooted hair and in original clothes. Marks: CLODREY/MADE IN FRANCE. (Courtesy Shirley Merrill)

14″ "Boys of Brittany" made by the Philippe Poupees et Creations Regionales of France. They have changable clothes with extra outfits sold separately so the costumes may be changed. Sleep eyes, rooted hair and all vinyl. The quality of these dolls is excellent. 1978.

"LaFamille Bella." The members of this French family are all rather large with the mother being 15″, and the Father about 16″. They are extremely fine quality and the parents have extra joints (see following photos). They are boxed together as if standing in front of a house. (Courtesy Phyllis Teague)

Mother of the French Family holds the baby who is fully jointed and has a flange neck joint. (Courtesy Phyllis Teague)

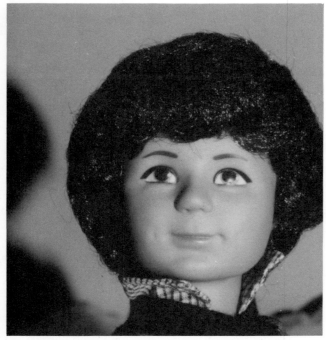

The Father of the French Family is the only member of the group that is smiling. He has painted blue eyes and dimples. The Brother from the French family looks just like his Father and even has light dimples and the same color hair. His eyes are painted blue. (Courtesy Phyllis Teague)

The Sister from the French Family has blue painted eyes and rather a downcast expression. (Courtesy Phyllis Teague)

Pierre Cardin of Paris designed outfits for the Effe firm of France during 1981 and 1982. The dolls were available in 15″, 18″ and 21″ sizes. The dolls will be marked: EFFE/MADE IN FRANCE.

12″ Socket head on five piece body which is made of a light weight plastic simular to celluloid. Marks: A TURTLEMARK IN A DIAMOND 32/34 on head. TURTLEMARK IN A DIAMOND and "34" on back. Has inset glass eyes, coin earrings and is original. The original box is yellow with colorful drawings of ethnic children holding hands on the sides. The top has: SCHILDKROT/PUPPEN/TURTLEMARK IN A DIAMOND. IN ALLER WELT 4783/34/29 MADE IN WESTERN GERMANY. (Courtesy June Schultz)

8″ Hummel. All vinyl, except torso. All original with open/closed mouth, painted features and molded hair in pigtails. Metal tag on hand with large V and bee. Other side of tag: AUS-DEM HUMMELERCK. Doll is marked: #1802 V WITH BEE M.J. HUMMEL/1966 W. GOBEL on head. Body is marked: HUM 1800 W. GOBEL/W. GERMANY. (Courtesy Austin Collection)

12″ "Wanderbub, the Traveler" and "Sticklies1" with knitting needles and cloth. All original. Deeply molded hair, painted features. ca. pre-1970's. (Courtesy Louise Nixon)

10″ All vinyl native with molded hair, loin cloth and necklaces and bracelets. Painted features. Marks: TURTLE IN A DIAMOND. MADE IN GERMANY. (Courtesy Nancy Lucas)

13″ "Alice in Wonderland." Same description as the Cinderella doll below. Made by Kehagias (Greece) and as with other doll, appears to be taken from an Alexander mold.

13″ "Cinderella" of the Fairy Tale Series by Kehagias (Greece). All good quality vinyl. Sleep blue eyes/lashes. Good quality clothes. Rooted hair is heavy and above average quality. Doll not marked. Paper tag and box read: KEHAGIAS. Appears to be taken from a Madame Alexander mold.

9½″ "American." Dolls of Nations. Made in Greece by Kehagias. Plastic body with vinyl head and limbs. Sleep blue eyes/lashes. Heavily painted lips. Good quality clothes with pantaloons and gown with attached slip. Has lace shawl and cap. No marks on doll, but has tag on wrist. Very similar to an Alexander doll and shown for information.

12″ Early 1950's Furga made of ceramic-like, very heavy plastic. Dark skin tones, mohair wig, sleep blue eyes, red fingernails. Has no talker mechanism in back, as dolls from the Furga company usually do. Original clothes.

23″ Marked: SEBINO/MADE IN ITALY on head and body. Plastic body and legs with vinyl arms and head. Blue sleep eyes with long lashes, open/closed mouth with two painted upper teeth and rooted blonde hair. Battery operated talker with record player. Record is in Italian and is marked: SEBINO 17-F. All original clothes.

22″ "Martina" of 1974 made by Furga of Italy. All original. Pink satin hoop skirt dress and cape trimmed with white maribou. Black velvet necklace with rhinestone ring on neck. Blonde rooted hair in upswept hairdo and ringlette curls over ears. (Courtesy Ann Wencel)

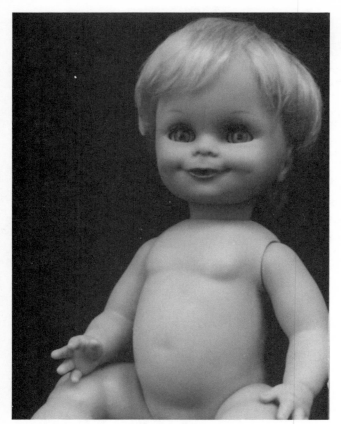

16″ Sexed boy doll with sleep blue eyes, open mouth/nurser and blonde rooted hair. Plastic body with vinyl head and limbs. Marks: SEBINO/MADE IN ITALY on head and body as well as ":57" on body. (Courtesy Carol Friend)

14″ "Lisa." Marks: ITALY Z.Z. on back. Distributed by F.W. Woolworth Co. Plastic with vinyl head and limbs. Sleep blue eyes and rooted blonde hair. (Courtesy Carol Friend)

17″ "Antonietta." Plastic and vinyl with inset eyes/lashes. Original. Has white plastic stand marked: FURGA. Doll is marked: 31232, FURGA, in a square, on head. A second doll just like this one only dressed in print gown, is called "Agnese". (Courtesy Treasure Trove)

17″ "Old Fashioned Girl." Plastic with vinyl arms and head. Inset brown eyes, painted lashes and freckles. Posable head. Very pretty hands with slender fingers with 2nd and 3rd fingers molded together. This is a "different" Furga face. Marks: FURGA/ITALY/31232, on head. 1977-78.

4½″ Nippon baby that is marked: NIPPON. Painted bisque with painted slant eyes, two painted upper teeth and on five piece bisque body with bent baby legs, painted on black shoes. Original silk outfit. Braid head band with jet and red beads. Original box. (Courtesy Glorya Woods)

24″ Italy's Zanini & Zambelli called "Nouvelle Vogue #67 Odette." Mod. 400. Cloth body with rigid vinyl legs to just above knees and modeled on shoes. Cloth arms to elbows with beautifully modeled hands. Excellent quality clothing. Rooted hair and oil painted features. Rigid vinyl socket head fits into cloth body. 1979.

7″ All bisque with molded painted hair, painted eyes. Molded and painted clothes with girl holding doll, boy holding slate. Both marked: MADE IN JAPAN. Shown with a Hull vase made about 1940. (Courtesy Glorya Woods)

4″ small turned wood, handpainted and made in Japan. Has extremely tiny little dolls in cut out eyes with one being green and the other red. (Courtesy Sally Freeman)

Left to right: 6″ Painted bisque with molded blonde hair, painted eyes, tiny mouth, jointed shoulders, with rest made in one piece. Marked: MADE IN JAPAN. 5″ bisque head with molded hair, painted eyes, papier mache five piece body with fingers not well defined. Marked: NIPPON. 2½″ Quints of painted bisque, jointed only at the shoulders, painted eyes and hair, marked: JAPAN. Original came in flimsy cloth bunting. 5″ Flower girl with molded hair and painted eyes, jointed only at the shoulders. Molded on white undies, painted on brown shoes. marked: MADE IN JAPAN. (Courtesy Glorya Woods)

4½″ "Professor Pook" of the "Mini-Martian" series made by J. SWEDLIN, INC. and MADE IN JAPAN., which are also the marks on the doll. Made in 1967 with others in the set: Mini, Bonnie, Meri and Teenie. Glasses are painted on white vinyl head. One piece body and limbs. Original coat and clothes under the coat are painted on the vinyl.

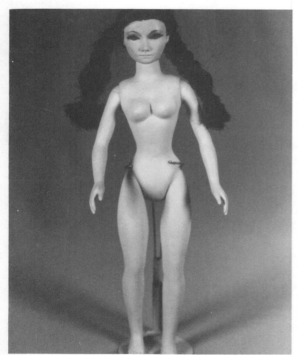

14″ marked: "MUNECAS VICTORIA/HECHA EN MEXICO", on head. Excellent quality, all vinyl, Indian looking eyes and brown skin tones with black rooted hair. Adult body with excellent detail of fingers and toes. (Courtesy Jayn Allen)

Close up of the 14″ doll marked: "MUNECAS VICTORIA/HECHA EN MEXICO" on head. The eyes are painted and the eye lids are molded. The hair is rooted. (Courtesy Jayn Allen)

14″ Boy and girl. Plastic body with vinyl head and limbs that look like wax. Sleep brown eyes, light freckles and very little nose and mouth detail. Marks: FAMOSA/MADE IN SPAIN, on head. His name is "Godo" and she is "Cloe." (Courtesy Anita Pacey)

8″ pair of Klumpe character men. Both are all original. The Klumpe dolls are made in Spain, and have a wire armature, posable body covered with material, round painted eyes and deep inverted "V" eyebrows. (Courtesy Pat Timmons)

8″ Group of Klumpe dolls made in Spain. All have elongated heads, deep inverted brows and are all original. Wire armature, cloth covered bodies. (Courtesy Pat Timmons)

7½" Nurse made with wire armature that is cloth covered and posable; on the style of the Klumpe dolls. Tag: CREACIONS GOYA/MADE IN SPAIN. The head is round with a hard finish and hand painted.

13" Marked: FAMOSA. Plastic body with vinyl head, arms and legs. Very pale brown sleep eyes with long lashes, freckles and rooted reddish blonde hair. Redressed. Closed smile mouth. Made in Spain ca. 1968.

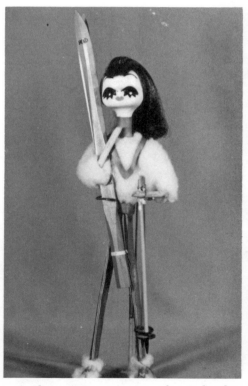

14" Skier. Wire armature that is leather covered. The head is plastic with very heavy molded lashes and hair lashes over that. Glued-on hair. Wood poles and skis. Tag: MADE IN SWITZERLAND/ EXPRESSLY FOR/SAKS FIFTH AVENUE. Doll was a gift from Betty Tait.

7" Goya bull fighter and 9" long bull. Tag: CREACIONS/MADE IN SPAIN/BARCELONA ESPANA. Very much like the Klumpe dolls, especially in the eyebrows, except the spacing is wider, and the head is round, covered with hard material. (Courtesy Diane Hoffman)

4½" tall Halloween "Flying Witch." All plastic with arms jointed only. String goes through middle of doll and as string is pulled the witch rides up and down with her arms turning in circles. Marks: NO. 9356/FUN WORLD INC./NEW YORK NY/MADE IN HONG KONG, inside arm. Gift from Bourgious family.

12" "Butch Cavendish" with his horse "Smoke." Full action figure. This doll is the "arch-villian" of the Lone Ranger series. 1978. (Courtesy Renie Culp)

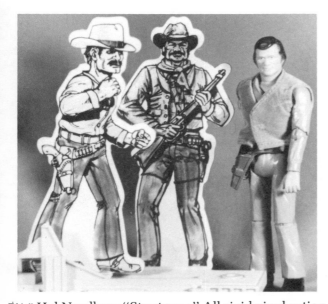

7¼" Hal Needham "Stuntman." All rigid vinyl action figure with vinyl hands and head. Vest removable only. Unique modelling in that upper chest and head is inset into molded body and moves together. Excellent quality and detail. Cardboard figures are 8" tall. Stand doll onto stand and he is "triggered" to knock down figures. Marks: 1977/HAL NEEDHAM & GABRIEL/PAT. PENDING.

Close up and good likeness of professional stuntman Hal Needham.

The first "Dennis the Menace" is same as shown in other photo but is unmarked (left). Center: 15″ Stuffed vinyl with one piece body and limbs, molded yellow hair, inset eyes, freckles. Original overalls. Marks: DENNIS THE MENACE, on neck and overalls. Right: 14″ All cloth, one piece body and limbs with vinyl head, molded yellow hair and painted features, freckles. Unmarked. (Courtesy Jeannie Mauldin)

12″ "Robert Vaughn" from the Man From U.N.C.L.E. Molded hair and painted features. Plastic and vinyl. Marks: "K-78". His friend, Illya Kuryakin, played by David McCallum, is marked: "K50." Information on box: 1965 METRO-GOLDWYN-MAYER INC./A.C. GILBERT CO.

Close up of the 15″ Dennis The Menace with inset brown eyes and very deeply molded open/closed mouth. (Courtesy Jeannie Mauldin)

14″ "Dennis The Menace." Stuffed vinyl with one piece body and limbs, molded on undies, dimples at knees and elbow and separate large toes. Thumb and small finger are also separate. Molded yellow hair with top knot in back. Eyebrows are painted on hair. Freckles and painted features. Original clothes. Marks: DENNIS THE MENACE/H.K.K./1958. MADE BY HALL SYND. INC. (Courtesy Kimport Dolls)

Second set of Hallmark dolls, all cloth with printed on detail and features. Some have one piece of clothing that is removable. Chief Joseph, Amelia Earhart, George Washington Carver, Babe Ruth, Susan B. Anthony and Annie Oakley.

The 1975 Hasbro catalog shows three action figures, left to right: "Jungle Survival" using a blonde G.I. Joe, center is a most unusual faced figure called "Secret Agent". Note hair, eye modeling and mustache. The third is "Emergency Rescue."

12″ "G.I. Joe" as frogman on sea sled and part of the "Adventurer Series." Front of sled has "G.I.JOE" imprinted on it, and the underside of the back is marked: OFFICIAL G.I. JOE SEA SLED/PATENT PENDING/HASBRO 1966. MADE IN U.S.A. This outfit is shown in the 1973 mail order catalogs. The sled is battery operated and actually dives. The original box is marked: 1966. Overall size of sled is 17″.

The basic "Defender" figure made by Hasbro in 1975. He is 11½″ tall and has straight arms and legs. At right are the different outfits: *Sniper Patrol, Commando Assault, Counter Attack, Forward Observer, Ambush* and *Point Man.*

G.I. Joe not included.

G.I. Joe not included.

7308 Uniform Assortment - The Action Team suits up in survival gear to complete dangerous missions and emergency rescues! Authentically styled with attention to detail. Assortment includes 6 each of the following: "Desert Survival"™ - Shirt, pants, belt, canteen; "Dangerous Mission"™ - Jungle green shirt, pants, rifle; "Fight for Survival"™ - Brown pants, shirt, machete; "Secret Rendezvous"™ - Gray parka, pants, flare gun; "Hidden Treasure"™ - Khaki shirt, pants, folding shovel; "Copter Rescue"™ - Zippered blue flight suit, binoculars.

7309 "Uniform Assortment" - Action gear for more daring escapades! Authentically styled with attention to detail. Assortment includes six each of the following: "Secret Mission"™ - Black jacket, khaki pants, pistol; "Danger Climb"™ - Green jump suit, climbing pick, rope; "Jungle Ordeal"™ - Camouflage jump suit, jungle knife; "Photo Reconnaissance"™ - Zippered jump suit, camera; "Desert Explorer"™ - Khaki bush jacket, shorts, pants; "Undercover Agent"™ - Trench coat, belt, walkie-talkie (Pants not included). 1975.

7280 "Land Adventurer"™; 7281 "Sea Adventurer"™; 7282 "Air Adventurer"™ - Completely assembled G.I. Joe mannequin with new Kung Fu Grip, life-like hair and beard, authentically designed uniform, boots, insignia and rifle; 7284 "Man of Action" - Completely assembled mannequin with new Kung Fu Grip, life-like hair, fatigue uniform, boots, insignia, rifle; 7283 "Black Adventurer" - Completely assembled mannequin with Kung Fu Grip, life-like hair, uniform, boots, insignia and rifle; 7290 "Talking Commander" - Completely assembled mannequin with Kung Fu Commander" - Completely assembled mannequin with Kung Fu Grip, life-like hair and beard, uniform, boots, insignia and rifle. One of eight different commands can be activated by pulling his dog tag; 7291 "Talking Black Commander" - Same featurers as 7290; 7292 "Talking Man of Action" - Completely assembled G.I. Joe mannequin with new Kung Fu Grip, life-like hair. Authentically designed fatique uniform, boots, insignia, rifle. One of eight different adventure commands can be activated by simply pulling his dog tag. 1975.

The Madame Hendren dolls were just a part of a long list of names used by Georgene Averill, which included Averill Mfg. Co., Georgene Novelty, Paul Averill Mfg. Co. and Madame Georgene Dolls. Both the Madame Hendren and Madame Averill dolls were produced by the Brophey Doll Co. in Canada. These firms made dolls of bisque, composition and a great many in cloth.

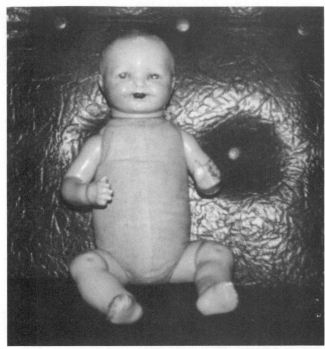

18″ Cloth body with composition head, arms and legs. Molded hair, sleep eyes, smiling open mouth with two upper teeth, tongue and dimples, Marks: MADAME HENDREN DOLL on head. Made during the time the Effanbee doll "Bubbles," and the Horsman doll "Dimples" were so popular. ca. 1926. (Courtesy Jeannie Mauldin)

Doll on left is 13½″ "Dimmie." 1929. All composition with a swivel waist that is ball jointed, very bent left arm, molded painted hair and very large eyes painted to the side. Romper suit is blue floral with white trim and she has a matching bonnet with lace around front edge. The shoes are stamped MADE IN GERMANY. Doll is stamped MDM. HENDREN. Right: 13″ and marked: MAXINE DOLL CO. All original and composition and does not have a swivel waist. (Courtesy Kay Bransky)

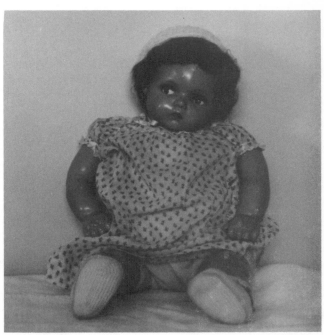

21″ "Baby Georgene." Cloth body with composition head, legs and arms. Mohair wig, with molded curly hair under wig. Gray eyeshadow and flirty sleep eyes. This same doll also came without flirty eyes. Dress old, but may not be original. This doll is unmarked, but there are some that are marked: BABY GEORGENE. Note hands with all fingers curled into the palms. (Courtesy Evelyn Samec)

12″ "Peterkin Indian." The same doll was used for "Betsy" and "Tommy Peterkin" in 1915. This same doll was also used as the Dolly Dingle, and Campbell Kids. Suntan color painted composition head and limbs with stuffed cloth body. Closed "watermelon" style mouth and painted eyes. All original. (Courtesy Kay Bransky)

18″ "Mama" doll of the 1920's. Cloth body with composition lower arms and legs and shoulderplate head. Sleep blue eyes, open mouth with two teeth and brown mohair wig. Voice box in body patented by B.E. Lloyd. Marks: E.I.H. and V D G, upside down in shoulderplate. (Courtesy Nancy Lucas)

11″ "Body Twist" doll by Horsman. All composition with painted, molded hair, eyes painted to side and has painted-on black shoes. ca. 1929-1930. (Courtesy Sylvia Bryant)

The 11″ Horsman "Body Twist" doll with dress which may be original. (Courtesy Sylvia Bryant)

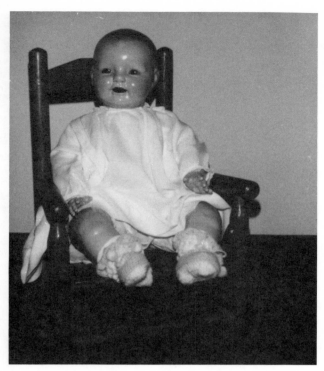

25″ "Baby Dimples." Cloth body with composition head, arms and very fat legs with upper part cloth. Made from 1928 to 1933. Smiling mouth that is open with two upper teeth. Sleep tin eyes and yellow lightly molded, painted yellow hair. Marks: E.I.H. CO. INC. on back of head. (Courtesy Jeannie Mauldin)

19″ "Bright Star." All composition with brown tin sleep eyes, brown human hair wig and all original. Tag: HORSMAN'S BRIGHT STAR. Doll is unmarked. ca. 1937. In 1952 Horsman used the name "Bright Star" for a hard plastic girl with open mouth and a saran wig. (Courtesy Dorothy Mulholland)

16″ "Chubby Baby" of 1942. Cloth body with composition should plate and head (swivel neck), arms and legs. Marks: HORSMAN on head. Shown in original pink flannel sacque with zipper in front and hood. Underneath is a flannel sleeper that is footed and has buttons at waist. Molded hair and sleep brown eyes. (Courtesy June Schultz)

15½″ Molded hair "Ruthie" that is all early stuffed vinyl. Also sold as "Fairy Skin Doll." One piece body and legs. Disc jointed arms. Blue sleep eyes, original clothes. 1953. Marks: HORSMAN on head. (Courtesy Mrs. Frank Miller)

15″ "Gold Medal Boy" of 1955. Deeply molded detailed hair, sleep blue eyes/lashes with painted lashes under the eyes. One piece stuffed vinyl body and limbs with wire through legs so doll can sit. Marks: 93/HORSMAN, on head. Not original.

12″ "Gold Medal Baby" All vinyl with one piece body and limbs. Molded hair, sleep blue eyes with hair lashes, open/closed mouth. Marks: HORSMAN on head. Not original clothes. 1957.

15″ 1957 version of "Cindy Kay" with early stuffed vinyl body and legs in one piece. Metal disc jointed stuffed arms, rooted blonde hair, sleep eyes/lashes. Marks: HORSMAN/82 1957, on head. (Courtesy Margaret Mandel)

Right: 25″ baby with plastic body and limbs and vinyl head with molded hair, sleep blue eyes and open/closed mouth. Jointed at neck, shoulders, elbows, hips and knees. Has 2nd and 3rd fingers molded together on left hand. Very much like doll shown with her, which is Ideal's "Bye Bye Baby." One on right is marked: HORSMAN, on back of head. (Courtesy Jeannie Mauldin)

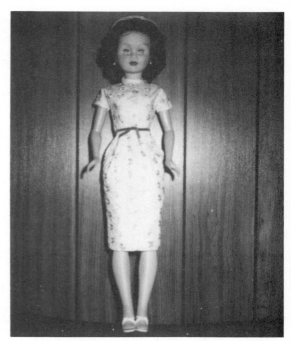

25" "Jacqueline Kennedy." Rigid vinyl body and limbs with delicate looking arms and hands. Vinyl head with rooted dark hair and sleep eyes. Original dress and earrings. High heel feet. Marks: HORSMAN/1961/J.K. 25/4. (Courtesy Ann Wencel)

This Jacqueline is shown in another outfit and the head is marked: HORSMAN/1961/JK 7 25. She is dressed in white sheath with lavender and pink print, green velvet belt, white high heel shoes, silk stockings, white pillbox hat and is wearing a necklace and earrings of pearls. (Courtesy Phyllis Lemanski)

18" "Mommy's Darling." Cloth with vinyl head and limbs. Left thumb, index and second finger molded together. The right 3rd finger is deeply curled into palm. 1967. Marks: 27 38/18 EYE/14/HORSMAN/67, on head. Tag: MADEMOISELLE DOLLS, on one side; SEAL OF QUALITY, on other. Sleep blue eyes/lashes and open/closed mouth. Original pale yellow organdy over yellow satin attached slip. Lace trimmed. (Courtesy Marjorie Uhl)

18" Black version of the other "Mommy's Darling" of 1967. See other photo for basic description. This model is a toddler with straight legs and all fingers are spread on both hands. (Courtesy Marjorie Uhl)

8″ "Country Kids." Plastic and vinyl with painted eyes, rooted hair and marked: HORSMAN DOLL INC./1976, on heads. Box: #2080 and IRENE SZOR DESIGN. Both are all original. (Courtesy Renie Culp)

13″ "Celeste Bride." Plastic with vinyl arms and head. Sleep blue eyes/lashes, open/closed mouth and has 2nd and 3rd fingers on left hand molded together. All others are separate. Marks: 29/HORSMAN DOLLS, INC./1977, on head. Original. Box: IRENE SZOR DESIGN. (Courtesy Treasure Trove)

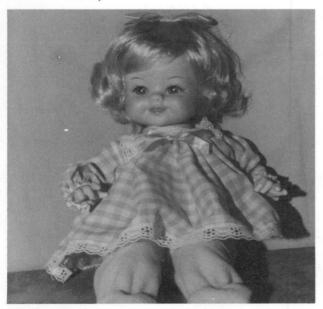

16″ "Baby Laugh & Cry." Laughs when picked up and cries when laid down. Battery operated. Cloth body with vinyl head and limbs. Painted eyes and original outfit of footed pink flannel and pink/white check top with lace trim. Pink ribbon in hair. Thumb holds index and 2nd finger on left hand with 3rd finger deeply curled into palm and finger slightly curled on right hand. 1978. (Courtesy Phyllis Teague)

23″ "Softy Skin." One piece body and limbs of dublon. The head is vinyl with rooted hair, sleep blue eyes/lashes. Open mouth/nurser. Marks: 4255/15 EYE/53/HORSMAN DOLLS, INC./1972, on head; G/HORSMAN INC. on back. Marketed to 1978. Original outfit. (Courtesy Phyllis Teague)

18″ "Lovely Softy Skin" of 1978. Marks: 13 (in squares)/ HORSMAN, on head. Vinyl head with rooted hair, sleep eyes/lashes and open mouth/nurser. One piece body and limbs of dublon. Original white outfit with lace trim. (Courtesy Phyllis Teague)

12″ "Angelove" by Hallmark and made by Horsman Dolls. Plastic body and legs with vinyl head and arms. Rooted hair and painted blue eyes. Marks: HORSMAN DOLLS INC/1974, on head, HORSMAN DOLLS INC, on back. Marketed to 1978.

15″ "Baby Squeezums." 1978. One piece soft vinyl stuffed body and limbs. Uses a basic head of the "Angelove" doll with full wig and eyes painted differently. Has three long painted lashes at sides of eyes. Dressed in red suedette with ecru sleeves and pinafore with red trim and hat.

24″ "Pudgie Baby" with plastic body and vinyl head and limbs. Rooted hair, sleep eyes, open mouth and has all fingers and toes separate. Marks: HORSMAN DOLL CO. 1980, on head; HORSMAN DOLLS INC. on back. All original in pink dress with lace trim, white socks tied with pink ribbons. Name used for 12″ doll in 1978. (Courtesy Jeannie Mauldin)

16″ "Snuggle Softee" dolls of 1978. Cloth bodies, limbs except guantlet style hands of vinyl. Vinyl head with rooted hair, painted eyes and came in assorted outfits.

8″ "Cinderella" of 1981 shown in the original box that came with the four Disney dolls.

The Horsman 1981 Disney dolls are all 8″ tall and came in a window style box with gold trim, made like a book. Dolls include "Snow White," "Alice in Wonderland," "Mary Poppins" and "Cinderella."

# Ideal Doll Company

In 1902 Morris Michtom formed the Ideal Toy and Novelty Company to produce his Teddy Bear and by 1915 the company was well established and led the industry. In the early 1930's Ideal leadership was in the hands of the founder's son, Benjamin F. Michtom, and during this time Mollye Goldman convinced the company that they should produce the Shirley Temple doll and she would design the clothes for the dolls. Production and sales of the Shirley Temple dolls of the 1930's has never been topped by any other doll, yet the most desirable and hardest to find doll produced by Ideal is the Judy Garland as Dorothy from the Wizard of Oz. To the collector a great many Ideal dolls are very collectable and a full collection could be built from this one company. See "Shirley Temple" section right after "Ideal" section.

# Bits and Pieces of Information

Some collectors think the "National Velvet" doll represents Elizabeth Taylor, but it is actually modeled after Lori Martin who played the part on the N.B.C. series. Made in sizes 30″ and 38″ in 1961. Elizabeth Taylor made the movie during the 1940's and the doll would have been in composition rather than plastic and vinyl.

The P-93 Toni dolls began to be called "Sara Ann" and "Sarah" and they will have saran glued-on wigs, where the Toni has the usual nylon hair that can be curled by the make-believe Toni wave sets. It was about this time that the American Character Doll Company picked up the use of the name "Toni" and began using it for their dolls called "Toni Sophisticates."

Betty Tait sent information that she had purchased a Kissy doll 22″ tall which has a hard plastic body and arms, jointed wrists and vinyl hands, plus has a vinyl head and legs. Her doll has *bent baby legs* and her face is different than the conventional Kissy dolls with thinner lips, different mold and expression. Her doll has original short curly reddish hair that is rooted, blue sleep eyes and is marked: IDEAL TOY CORP./K-21-L-1, on head and IDEAL TOY CORP. K-22 US Pat. No. 3,054,215 and not the usual Pat. Pend.

The 1957 Ideal Company catalog shows the Revlon doll offered in sizes 18″, 20″, 23″ and 26″. This same catalog shows the 10½″ using the Little Miss Revlon's body and a more teen style face with dimples as "Crown Princess." Each of these dolls came with a tiara and were available in basic black chemise of lace, plus clothes that could be purchased separately. A 10½″ size was offered with lace gown and fur trimmed cape. This same dressed doll was offered in the 18″ size (Revlon doll) also. A doll 10½″ was available in a box with wardrobe and also a travel case was offered with the imprint of a four point crown on the front. Ideal tried, unsuccessfully, to produce this same doll as "Teen Age Shirley Temple" in 1958.

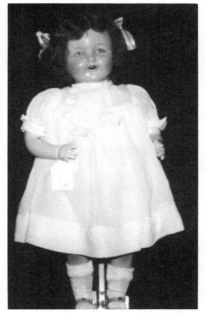

22″ "Pretty Peggy." 1930. Cloth body, straight composition legs, bent composition arms with open hands and 2nd and 3rd fingers molded together and slightly curled. Flirty sleep eyes in composition head and open/closed smiling mouth. Has four painted upper teeth. Marcelled mohair brown wig. Marks: IDEAL, in diamond, along with U.S.A., on head. (Courtesy Jeannie Mauldin)

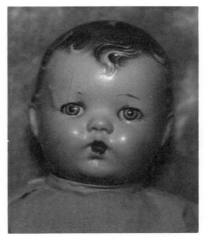

13″ "Cuddles" of 1932. Cloth body and legs with composition head and arms. Molded hair, sleep tin eyes and not original. Marks: IDEAL DOLL/ MADE IN U.S.A., on head. This doll was made up to 1938. (Courtesy Shirley Merrill)

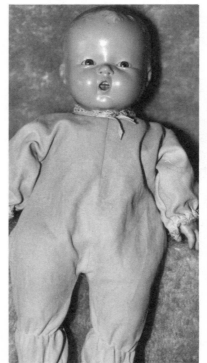

16″ "Snoozie." Cloth body and upper limbs with composition head and lower limbs. Green celluloid over tin sleep eyes, molded hair. The hands are replaced, as original were all rubber. Marks: B. LIPFERT, on head. Made for Ideal Doll and Toy Corp. 1933. The mouth is yawning and has molded tongue. (Courtesy Shirley Merrill)

The 1934 *Needlecraft* magazine offered this 14″ "Sallykins" for selling three subscriptions, plus an extra 50 cents. Cloth body with composition head and legs. The arms were rubber, flirty, sleep smiling eyes, open mouth with two upper and two lower teeth, also has dimples just below the mouth level. Dressed in organdy with lace trim. Doll will be unmarked or have IDEAL, in a diamond on head.

15″ "Ginger Bride." Box is marked: IDEAL in oval and has pictures of little girls at play. Doll is all composition with mohair wig and sleep eyes. Mark: (X), on head. Has a blotted-out "Shirley Temple" on back. Doll has open mouth with upper teeth. ca. 1939. (Courtesy Marge Meisinger)

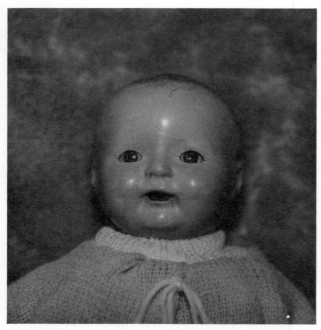

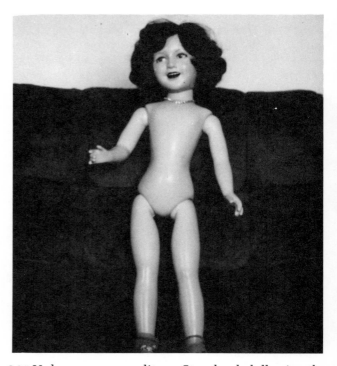

14″ "Hush A Bye Baby." 1935. Cloth body and legs with composition head and arms. Grey celluloid over tin sleep eyes, molded hair and open mouth. Dimples. Marks: IDEAL in a diamond, on head. Had four upper teeth. (Courtesy Shirley Merrill)

24″ Unknown personality or Storybook doll using the Deanna Durbin doll. May be a Snow White. All composition with open smiling mouth/teeth, sleep blue eyes and original black human hair wig. Only remains of clothes are hose and gold sandals. Marks: IDEAL/25, on body. ca. 1939-1941. (Courtesy Evelyn Samec)

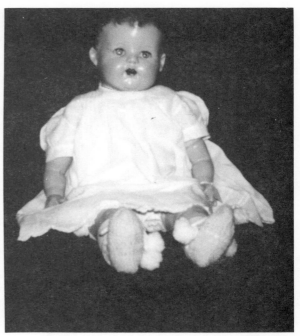

Left: 21″ "Deanna Durbin." Marked on head: DEANNA DUR-BIN/IDEAL DOLL, and on body: IDEAL DOLL. Dark brown mohair wig, blue-green sleep eyes, open mouth with six teeth. All composition. Right is all composition "Judy Garland" teen doll that is 21″ and marked on head: IDEAL-MADE IN U.S.A., and on back: IDEAL DOLL, along with a backward 21. Light brown human hair wig, brown sleep eyes, open mouth with four teeth. 1939-1941. (Courtesy Glorya Woods)

20″ "Honey Baby" of 1943. Cloth body with composition head and limbs. Molded, painted brown hair, sleep blue eyes, open mouth with molded tongue and two upper teeth. Marks: IDEAL DOLL/MADE IN U.S.A., on head. (Courtesy Jeannie Mauldin)

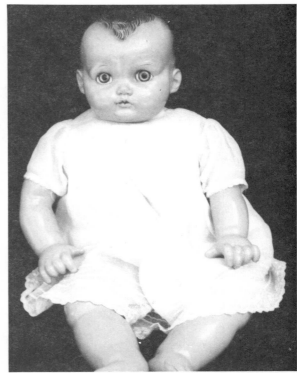

13″ World War II Soldier. All composition with mold-ed hair, painted large black eyes to the side, painted smile mouth. He is on a Shirley Temple mold body and in original clothes with cap missing. Marks: IDEAL DOLL U.S.A., on head, and U.S.A. 13, on back. ca. 1942. (Courtesy Jeannie Mauldin)

21½″ Marked: IDEAL DOLL/MADE IN USA/PAT. NO. 2252077. Stuffed cloth body with composition head and limbs. Brown molded, painted hair, blue sleep eyes. This same mold us-ed on latex body later and called "Magic Squeezums." Head was also used with less rounded eyes in hard plastic with a shoulder plate. ca. 1940's. (Courtesy Edith Evans)

The 1951 "Judy Splinters" Doll came in three sizes: 18", 22" and 36". Cloth body with vinyl head and limbs. Large painted eyes and a wide open/closed mouth. Has yarn-like hair.

22" "Saucy Walker." All hard plastic with glued on black wig and has brown sleep eyes. Head turns as she walks. Marks: IDEAL DOLL, on head and body. 1951. The Black "Saucy Walkers" are very rare. (Courtesy Doris Chandler)

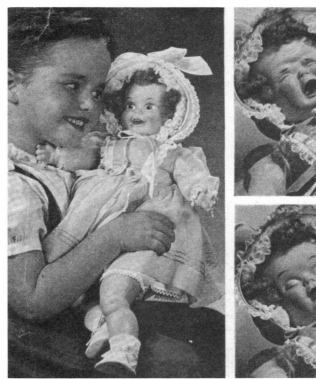

The Oct. 6, 1951 *Saturday Evening Post* carried an ad for Vinylite brand resins showing two Ideal dolls. One is pictured here: "Trilby," Ideal's magic 3-faced doll. The doll's head has three sides, one smiling, one sleeping and other crying and is worked by knob on top of the head. Cloth body with vinyl head and limbs.

21" "Toni." All hard plastic and marked "P-93." Has dark brown nylon hair. This same doll, if it has a saran wig, was called "Sara Ann" and "Sarah." Original clothes except shoes. The smaller doll is the regular P-90 size "Toni" so the comparision of sizes can be seen. She is also original, except shoes, and has black nylon wig (Author)

14" "Toni" marked: IDEAL DOLL P-90. One wears a brunette, the other a blonde nylon wig. Both dolls are all original. Dark hair one is in deep blue and white bodice dress with multi-color trim. Blonde is in red with white bodice and blue/red trim, blue buttons. (Author)

14" "Toni." All hard plastic with dark and platinum nylon wigs. Both in original tagged "Toni" dresses, which came in various prints with white attached apron and slip. Both have rose color skirts and white pinafore aprons with the dark hair one having blue floral trim and sleeves and light hair one yellow-gold floral print trim and sleeves marked "P-90". (Courtesy Ann Wencel)

21" "Toni" marked "P-93." All hard plastic with two platinum blondes and one red head all with nylon hair. Left and middle: Tops are pink, belts gold. Both have blue skirts with gold print with center one being more greenish blue. Both have matching purses. These polished cotton dresses are tagged. The right doll is in white cotton with pink and green flowers running up and down in rows, white rick rack around neck. It is also tagged. All have attached slips. (Courtesy Ann Wencel)

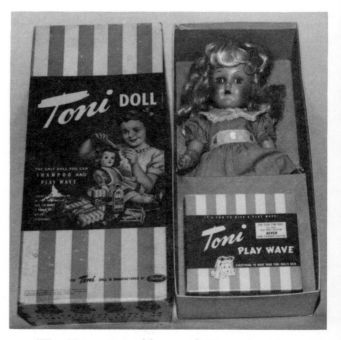

P-91 15" "Toni." All hard plastic with dark red and blonde nylon wigs. Both have pink silk dresses trimmed but differently on bodices; attached slips. Both dolls are mint in their boxes, but came without tags. (Courtesy Ann Wencel)

14" "Toni" in original box with Toni Play Wave set. Blonde nylon hair. Doll is all hard plastic, glued on wig, blue sleep eyes. Original dress is aqua with white lace and trim. Marks: IDEAL DOLL P-90. (Courtesy Pat Timmons)

19″ "Toni" pin hipped walkers. Marks: P-92 IDEAL DOLL MADE IN U.S.A. on head, IDEAL DOLL 19 on back. Dressed doll is original. Both are white blondes. The eyes on the walkers have a green shading and black eyeshadow. (Courtesy Ann Wencel)

16″ "Mary Hartline."All hard plastic walker, early vinyl head with rooted hair. Blue sleep eyes. 1952. Marks: "V-91," on head and IDEAL 16, on body. Off white dress with gold trim. Red lines and hearts and red boots with red and white ties. (Courtesy Virginia Jones)

16″ "Mary Hartline." All hard plastic; one on left being a doll that is strung, and one on right a pin hipped walker. The walker has a thinner face and legs. The walker is marked: IDEAL DOLL/MADE IN U.S.A., on head. On back: IDEAL DOLL-14. The strung doll marked: IDEAL P-91, on back, yet both dolls are 16″ tall. Both are all original. (Courtesy Ann Wencel)

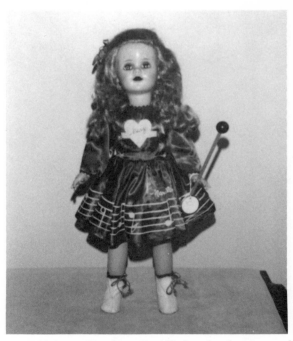

23″ "Mary Hartline." All hard plastic and original. Rayon silk dress, sleep eyes with black eyeshadow, glued on saran wig. Marks: IDEAL DOLL, on head. IDEAL DOLL P-94, on body. (Courtesy Ann Wencel)

15″ "Toni" in Red Cross Nurse uniform. All hard plastic with dark blonde wig, sleep eyes with dark eyeshadow. Unlike the "Miss Curitey" dolls, this dress is shorter and her cape has a front flip that had buttons on top. (Courtesy Ann Wencel)

21″ "Miss Revlon" in tagged dress called "Queen of Diamonds." Golden blonde rooted hair, blue sleep eyes, jointed waist, all vinyl. Jewelry consists of necklace, bracelet and rhinestone drop earrings. Dress is pink lace with flowered design, beige straw hat and a fur stole. Shown with original box. (Courtesy Betty Cossiboin)

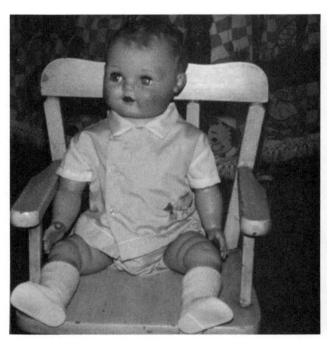

12″ Ideal Thrift Kit Doll. Strung hard plastic with side glancing sleep eyes, molded hair and marked: IDEAL DOLL on back. Not original. Was sold to put together and make clothes for. Late 1950's. In 1960-1961, came in an 8″ size called "Tiny Boy." (Courtesy Shirley Merrill)

23″ "Betsy Wetsy" of 1959. Plastic body with vinyl arms, legs and head with beautifully molded hair, sleep eyes, open/closed mouth, almost straight baby legs and open hands with all fingers separate. Arms are strung. Marks: IDEAL DOLL B-23, on head. Also came with rooted hair over molded. The mold used earlier was called "Baby Ruth" which had a cloth body with vinyl head and limbs. (Courtesy Jeannie Mauldin)

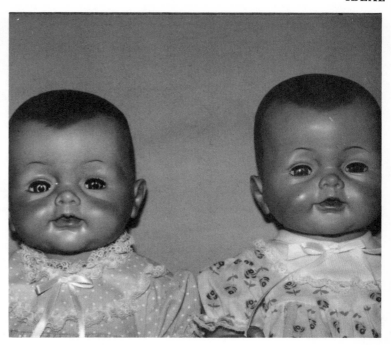

Full view of a 25″ "Bye Bye Baby" of 1960 showing detail of hands and bend of legs. The feet are as well detailed as the hands are. Will be marked: IDEAL TOY CORP/HB-25, on back and IDEAL TOY CORP., on head. (Courtesy Phyllis Teague)

Shows differences in two "Bye Bye" babies of 1960. 25″ plastic & vinyl with molded hair and sleep eyes, plus excellent detail to hands and feet as well as legs and arms. Open mouth/nurser. Doll on left has yellowish brown eyes and one on right has blue eyes. One on right also has a rounder, fatter head. (Courtesy Phyllis Teague)

32″ "Penny Playpal." All vinyl toddler with rooted hair, blue sleep eyes, open/closed mouth and has a molded tongue. Marks: IDEAL DOLL/32-E-L, on head and IDEAL, in oval, on back. Also came marked: B-32-B PAT. PEND. (Courtesy Shirley Merrill)

24″ "Susy Playpal" 1960-1961. Baby with plastic body and excellent detailed vinyl arms and legs. Fingers curled on left hand, right hand is open with 2nd and 3rd fingers molded together. Vinyl head with rooted hair, sleep eyes, smiling open mouth. Marks: IDEAL DOLL O.E.B.-24-3, on head. IDEAL, in oval, on back. Head and arms are strung. (Courtesy Jeannie Mauldin)

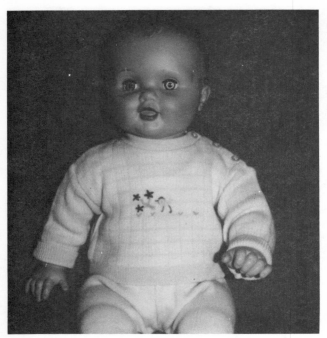

24″ "Betsy Wetsy." All vinyl and very chubby. Marks: IDEAL (in oval) 24-3, on body and B B 24-3/IDEAL DOLL, on head. Brown molded hair, sleep blue eyes/lashes. Has an open/closed mouth with molded tongue. 1960. (Courtesy Shirley Merrill)

8½″ "Pebbles" and "Bam Bam." Plastic bodies and legs with vinyl head and arms. Both have all fingers spread. She has an open/closed mouth and blue painted eyes to side. He has a closed mouth and brown painted eyes to the side. She wears plastic bone in hair, both have felt clothes. Marks: HANNA BARBARA PRODS, INC./ IDEAL TOY CORP./BB-8¼/1965, on Bam Bam. She is marked same except last line which is: FS-8¼/1965.

42″ "Daddy's Girl." Rooted dark brown hair, blue sleep eyes with lashes, closed mouth grin, has extra joints at waist and ankles. She came in 36″ and 42″ sizes to represent a 12-13 year old girl. 1960 and 1961 only. Marks: IDEAL TOY CORP./G-42-1. The 25″ and 30″ were marketed as Miss Ideal in 1961 and in 1962 were marketed as Miss Twist and Terry Twist. All original in red plaid dress, red hat and white collar. (Courtesy Kay Bransky)

Magazine ad reads "They're cool, they're 'in', they're go-go-goin'! The 24″ Jet Set Dolls are dressed the latest mod fashions and jewelry. Big bold colored knits, prints and see-thru plastic creations set off the striking beauty of each vinyl face. Their polyurethane bodies are incredibly poseable from the top of their washable, rooted Saran 'coifs' to the tips of their dancing shoes. Its a bloomin pleasure to introduce 'Stefanie', 'Chelsea' and 'Petula.' " 1967.

9″ "Baby Belly Button." Plastic and vinyl with green painted eyes, blonde hair, and closed smiling mouth. Original top. Marks: 1970 IDEAL TOY CORP./E9-5-H139/HONG KONG, on head; IDEAL TOY CORP./HONG KONG 2A-0156, on back. (Courtesy Shirley Merrill)

9″ "Baby Belly Button" with pale blue painted eyes, blonde rooted hair. Closed smile mouth. Not original. Marks: 1970 IDEAL TOY CORP./E9-1-H164/HONG KONG, on head and IDEAL TOY CORP./HONG KONG/2A-0156, on back. (Courtesy Shirley Merrill)

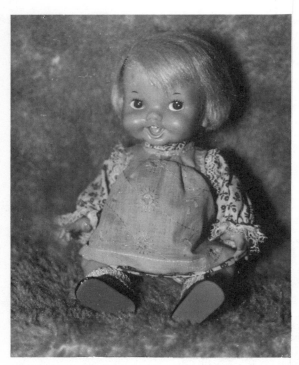

9″ "Baby Belly Button" with dark blue painted eyes, light blonde hair. Wide open/closed smiling mouth with molded tongue and two painted upper teeth. Not original. Marks: 1970 IDEAL TOY CORP./E9-5-H139/HONG KONG, on head. IDEAL TOY CORP./HONG KONG/2A-0156, on back. (Courtesy Shirley Merrill)

9″ "Baby Belly Button" with brown painted eyes straight ahead, bright orange rooted hair, original top and marked: 1970 IDEAL TOY CORP. /E9-1-H169/HONG KONG, on head. Marks are the same on back. (Courtesy Shirley Merrill)

# Crissy and Family

All information supplied by Karen Heidemann.

Crissy:

1969: 17½" Auburn hair, brown sleep eyes. Black doll with black hair and eyes. White doll dressed in orange lace dress. Growing hair reaches the feet or below. In later issues hair shortened to hips. One piece body. Black version wears apple-green lace dress.

1969-1970: Aqua dress and shoes. One piece body.

1970: Black "Crissy" in apple green dress, green shoes, one piece body, black hair and eyes.

1971: "Movin' Groovin' Crissy" in orange midi dress and boots, posing waist. Came in Black & White.

1971: "Talky Crissy" in long pink robe and shoes. Two talking models, one with string for talker on back, one on the side. Hair cropped differently than other dolls.

1972: "Look Around Crissy" in green plaid dress, green shoes. Black or White. Hair curly, less painted on makeup. Head and upper body turns from left to right.

1973: "Swirla Curler Crissy" in red plaid jumper dress with holly leaf on shoulder, red blouse and shoes. Black or White. Hair curly, less makeup at eyes. Curler device for hair.

1974: "Twirly Bead Crissy." White and pink check dress, white shoes, pink and white beads to use in hair. Hair curly and very little eye makeup. Came in Black or White.

1977: 19" "Hair Magic Crissy, has no pony tail, comes with five hair pieces. White camisole top and shoes, pink skirt, reddish hair and brown painted eyes, using the Tiffany Taylor body and shoes. Black or White.

# Velvet

1970: 15½" Crissy's cousin. Blonde hair, lavender sleep eyes. In Black or White.

1970-1971: Black "Velvet" in lavender corduroy and lavender shoes.

1970-1971: "Movin' Groovin' Velvet" in two tone pink, long waisted dress, purple bow on skirt in front and in hair, purple shoes, posing waist. Black or White.

1971: "Talking Velvet" in long yellow robe and shoes.

1972: "Look Around Velvet" in red plaid dress, white or red shoes, pull string in back. Head and upper body turn from left to right. Black or White.

1973: " Beauty Braider" in lavender floral dress and shoes. Comes with lavender braiding device for hair. Black or White.

1974: "Swirly Daisy" in purple, pink and green plaid dress with white front. Lavender shoes and daisy chain for hair. Black or White.

# Velvet's Little Sister, Later Called Cinnamon

1971: 11½" Tosca blonde hair, blue painted eyes, one piece body. Came dressed in orange polka dot shorts and sleeveless top and orange snub nose shoes.

1971: "Cinnamon" with hair doodler. Orange polka dot shorts and top with white yoke and orange shoes. Black or White.

1974: "Cinnamon" with Curly Ribbons. In blue bibbed shorts and checkered shirt, yellow and white curly ribbon hairdo dangle for hair, blue shoes on White doll as well as on Black.

# Velvet's Friends

1970-1971: "Mia." 15½" with black hair and blue sleep eyes. White doll only, dressed in blue bubble suit, blue shoes and has one piece body.

1972: "Diana," 15½" blonde hair, blue painted eyes, tanned skin and a butterfly tatoo on right knee. White doll only. Posing waist, lavender short suit (bibbed) and white lace up clogs.

# Crissy's Friends

1971: "Kerry" 17½". Blonde hair, green eyes, one piece body. White ony. Dressed in green elephant print short suit and green shoes.

1972: "Brandi" 17½" ash blonde, braids on sides of head, blue painted eyes, heart tatoo on right cheek, posing waist, orange jersey bathing suit and orange lace up clogs.

1969-1970: "Tressy." Black hair, sleep eyes, 17½", with one piece body. Skin tone is slightly tan, orange and white embossed printed Hawaiian dress and black shoes. White or Black. A Sears exclusive.

1971: "Posin' Tressy." 17½" black hair and blue sleep eyes. White only. Aqua silk short dress with white lace sleeves, aqua shoes. Also has a Brides dress, veil, panties and shoes.

1970-1971: "Cricket" 15½", red tosca blonde hair and brown eyes. Orange and white large check A-line dress, orange shoes and posing waist. White only.

1971: "Blue Eye Cricket" same as above except has blue sleep eyes. Not much is known about this doll. May have been a Sears exclusive. Dressed as above or in aqua Bride's Maid dress. White only.

1976: "Tara." 15½", Black only. Black sleep eyes, yellow and white check pants and top with white front on shirt, black braids on side of head with white bows, yellow shoes. One piece body.

# Baby Crissy

1973: 24" rooted auburn hair, brown eyes, hair grows from pull string in back. Dressed in pink layette dress and panties, no shoes. Later came in salmon dress and in 1975 in lavender.

1981: Re-introduced "Baby Crissy," see photo and description at end of "Crissy" section. The 1982 "Baby Crissy" had shoulder length curled up hair. A Toy trade magazine has a photo of a 20" "Baby Velvet" which is 4" shorter than the "Baby Crissy," but they may have never reached the store shelves, as none have been found by Crissy collectors.

This is the first "Crissy." 17½" with auburn hair, brown sleep eyes/lashes. 1968-1969. Orange lace dress, orange shoes. Hair to feet and below with later ones shortened to hip. Straight body. Marks: 1968/IDEAL TOY CORP/GH-17-H-129, on head. 1969/IDEAL TOY CORP./GH-18 U.S. PAT. PEND. #3,162,976, on hip. (Courtesy Karen Heidemann)

#1 Black "Crissy" with hair that flows onto the floor. Straight body. Marks: 1968/IDEAL TOY CORP/GH-17-H129, on head. 1969/IDEAL TOY CORP./GH-18 U.S. PAT. PEND. #3,162,976, on hip. Apple green lace dress. (Courtesy Ann Wencel)

Shows three "Crissys" Left: 1969. Orange lace dress, hair will go to feet or below, sleep brown eyes. Right: is "Crissy" in aqua dress and shoes, straight body, black hair and black sleep eyes of 1969-1970. Center is 1969-1970 Black "Crissy" in apple green dress, pink shoes, straight body and black hair and eyes. Marks same as other doll. (Courtesy Karen Heidemann)

1971 "Talking Crissy" in long pink robe and shoes. Pull string in back or on side. Hair cropped differently than other dolls. 1971 "Talky Velvet" in long yellow robe and shoes. Came with rollers, ribbons, hair brush, comb, bobby pins and bows. (Courtesy Karen Heidemann)

1971 "Movin' Groovin' Crissy" in orange midi dress and boots, posing, turning waist, has purple and orange yarn tie belt. Came with styling book and brush. Black and White. (Courtesy Karen Heidemann)

17½" 1971 "Kerry,". Blonde hair, green sleep eye/lashes, straight body, in White only. Green elephant print short suit and green shoes. Marks: 1970 IDEAL TOY CORP./NGH-18-H-172 HONG KONG, on head. 1969 IDEAL TOY CORP./GH 18-U.S.PAT #3162976, on hip. 11½" "Velvet's Little Sister," later called "Cinnamon." Tosca hair, blue painted eyes, straight body. Marks: 1971 IDEAL TOY CORP./GH-12-H-183 HONG KONG, on head. 1972 IDEAL TOY CORP./U.S.PAT 3162976, on back. Dressed in orange polka dot shorts and long top, orange "t" strap shoe. (Courtesy Karen Heidemann)

Black and White 1971 "Cinnamon" with hair doodler. Orange polka dot shorts and top with white yoke that has green bow, orange shoes. Painted eyes. (Courtesy Karen Heidemann)

1972 "Look Around Crissy" and "Velvet" in Black or White. "Crissy": Green plaid gown, green shoes, curly hair. Upper body turns with pull string. "Velvet": red plaid dress, white or red shoes, pull string, doll's upper body turns. (Courtesy Karen Heidemann)

17½″ "Crissy" in black wig and dressed in a separate gown sold for her called "Lemon Lite." Gown is yellow satin with bare back and trimmed with yellow fake fur. (Courtesy Karen Heidemann)

15½″ "Velvet," Crissy's Cousin. Blonde hair, lavender sleep eyes/lashes. White dolls: 1969-1970, purple velvet A-line dress and purple shoes. Later went to purple corduroy dress and purple shoes. Black doll: Lavender corduroy dress and lavender shoes. 1970-1971. (Courtesy Karen Heidemann)

1970-1971. "Movin' Groovin' Velvet." Dressed in two toned pink long waisted dress, purple bow on skirt and in hair, purple shoes, posing waist. In Black or White. Came with styling book and brush. (Courtesy Karen Heidemann)

California Cousins of Crissy. 15½″ "Dina." Blonde hair, blue painted eyes, tanned skin, butterfly tatoo on right knee. Posing waist, lavender short bibbed suit and white lace up clogs. MARKS: 1971 IDEAL TOY CORP./GHD-15-H-186 HONG KONG, on head. 1971 IDEAL TOY CORP./MG-15-U.S. PAT. 3162976/ OTHER PATS. PEND. HONG KONG ON BACK. "Brandi." 17½″ Ash blonde hair, blue painted eyes, heart tatoo on right cheek, posing waist, orange jersey bathing suit, orange lace up clogs. Marks: 1971 IDEAL TOY CORP./GHB-18-H-185 HONG KONG, on head. 1971 IDEAL TOY CORP. MG-18-U.S. PAT 3-162-978, on back. (Courtesy Karen Heidemann)

1971 *blue eyed* "Cricket", same as above except blue eyes. Assumed to be a Sears special. Posing waist and dressed in aqua Brides Maid gown or in same outfit as the other doll. Came in White only. Marks: 1970 IDEAL TOY CORP. 1970-1971 "Cricket." 15½". Red tosca hair and brown eyes/lashes. Orange and white large check A-line dress, orange shoes and posing waist. White only. Has orange ribbon belt.

1971 "Posin' Tressy." 17½". Black hair and blue sleep eyes, twist and turn waist. White only. Came in aqua silk short dress with white lace sleeves, aqua shoes. The Bride outfit was a Sears Gift Set. (Courtesy Karen Heidemann)

17½" "Tressy." 1969-1970. Black hair, blue sleep eyes/lashes. Straight body, skin tone slightly tanned. Orange and white embossed printed, Hawaiian print dress and black shoes. A Sears exclusive. Marks: 1969 IDEAL TOY CORP./GH-18-U.S. PAT. 3162976, on hip. 1970 IDEAL TOY CORP./SGH-17-HL6L/HONG KONG, on head. (Courtesy Karen Heidemann)

1973. 24" "Baby Crissy." Rooted deep auburn hair, brown sleep eyes, hair grows from pull string in back. Open/closed mouth with painted teeth. Marks: 1972 IDEAL TOY CORP./GHB-H-235, on head. 1973 IDEAL TOY CORP. /GHB 2M 2611 on back. In 1973 both Black and White versions came in pink, in 1974 came in either salmon on white, or green on white, 1975 both were in lavender. Came without shoes. (Courtesy Karen Heidemann)

1973 "Swirla Curler Crissy." Red plaid jumper dress with holly leaf on shoulder, with red blouse and shoes. Curler device for hair. Curly hair and very little makeup. Came in Black or White. Marks: 1968 IDEAL TOY CORP./GH-17-H-120, on head. 1968 IDEAL TOY CORP./GH 18 U.S. PAT. #3,162,976, on hip. (Courtesy Karen Heidemann)

15½″ "Velvet Beauty Braider." Lavender floral dress and lavender shoes. Came with lavender braiding device for hair. Available in Black or White. (Courtesy Karen Heidemann)

1974 "Velvet Swirly Daisy." Purple, pink and green plaid dress with white front. Lavender shoes and daisy chain for hair. Black or White. Marks: 1969 IDEAL TOY CORP./GH-15-H-157, on head. 1970 IDEAL TOY CORP./GH-15 2M516901, on right hip. (Courtesy Karen Heidemann)

1974 "Twirly Bead Crissy." White and pink check gown, white shoes, pink and white beads to use in hair. Curly hair and very little eye makeup. Came in Black or White. (Courtesy Karen Heidemann)

1974 "Cinnamon" with Curly Ribbons. Blue bibbed shorts and checkered shirt, yellow and white curly ribbon hairdo dangle for hair. Orange shoes on White doll and blue on the Black doll. Painted eyes. (Courtesy Karen Heidemann)

15½" "Tara" (Black only) 1976. Yellow and white checked pants and top with white front on shirt. Black braids on side of head with white bows, yellow shoes, straight body and marked: 1975 IDEAL TOY CORP./H 250 HONG KONG, on head. 1970 IDEAL TOY CORP./GH 15-2M516901, on hip. Shown with 15½" 1970-1971 "Mia." Black hair and blue sleep eyes/lashes. Blue romper style suit, blue shoes, straight body. White only. Marks: 1970 IDEAL TOY CORP./NGH-15-H173, on head. 1970 IDEAL TOY CORP./GH-15-2M516901, on hip. The "Tara" has been mistaken as a Black version of "Mia," but this is not so. (Courtesy Karen Heidemann)

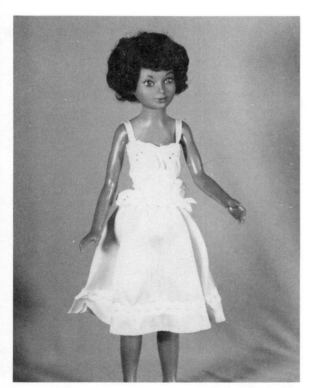

18" "Magic Hair Crissy." Plastic body, legs. Vinyl arms, head. Rooted hair with velour type dots for extra hair pieces. Lower torso is molded to the side. Hair attachments include: ribbon looped braids; ponytail with plastic head band marked "Crissy;" braids in twirls with plastic ball ends; twin ponytails. Marked: 1974/IDEAL, in oval/HOLLIS NY 11423/2-M-2854-01, on back. 1977/IDEAL TOY CORP./M.H.C.-19-H-281/ HONG KONG, on head.

1977 19" "Hair Magic Crissy." No pony tail, comes with five hair pieces. White camisole top and shoes, pink skirt, reddish hair and brown painted eyes. Came in Black or White. Doll is on a Tiffany Taylor's body and shoes. Marks: 1977 IDEAL TOY CORP/ M.H.C.-19-H-281/HONG KONG, on head. 1974 IDEAL, in oval/Hollis N.Y./11423/2M-5854-01, on hip. (Courtesy Karen Heidemann)

11½″ "Dorothy Hammill." Champion Ice Skater. All excellent quality with plastic body and hands. Vinyl head, arms and legs. Legs are bendable. Rooted brown hair and painted blue eyes. Open/closed mouth with painted teeth. Marks; 1977 DH/IDEAL, in oval, /H-282/HONG KONG. 1975 IDEAL, in oval/US PAT. NO. 3903640/HOLLIS NY 11423/HONG KONG P. Stand is marked: D H/177 IDEAL.

9″ "Suntan Dodi." Plastic body and legs, vinyl head and arms. Open/closed mouth with painted teeth. Painted eyes and rooted hair. Tans in sunlight returns to normal away from sunlight. (Also Sun-tan Tuesday Taylor and Eric) Marks: 1977 IDEAL, in oval/HOLLIS NY 11423, on hip. 1964/IDEAL TOY CORP./D)-9-5, on head. Ideal used this older head mold with a newer body.

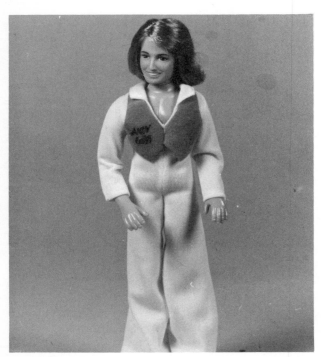

7″ "Andy Gibb." Rigid vinyl with vinyl head. Painted eyes, open/closed mouth with painted teeth. Center part, long hair. Original clothes, came with a dance stand. Marks: Row of numbers that can not be read/S.G.L. IDEAL in oval/H-317/HONG KONG, on head, and ANDY GIBB/IDEAL TOY CORP./HONG KONG, on lower back. 1978-1980 only.

12″ Black "Tuesday Taylor," Super Model. Marks: 1977 IDEAL H-293/HONG KONG P, on head. 1978 IDEAL HOLLIS N.Y./11423/HONG KONG P., on lower back. All vinyl posable doll. Painted eyes and rooted hair. Original. Many clothes were available for the doll which came in both Black and White. (Courtesy Renie Culp)

11½″ "Tuesday Taylor," Beauty Queen. She stands with magnetic shoes on a round disk stand. 1975. (Courtesy Renie Culp)

13″ "My Bottle Baby." Pull-string operated doll nods head as it drinks from bottle. "Milk" returns to bottle when removed from doll's mouth. Vinyl head with rooted hair and open mouth. Painted blue eyes. 1979. Came in either Black or White. Cloth body and arms. Material legs same as original skirt. Clothes are non-removable. By 1981 was called "Snuggle" with three faces, which also came in Black or White. (Courtesy Phyllis Teague)

1981 "Baby Crissy." 24″, tall in white with yellow trim. From the 1981 Ideal catalog. The 1982 catalog shows the same 15″ "Crissy" doll with red hair. 15″ "Velvet" of 1981, lavender sleep eyes and light blonde nylon hair, dressed in all white with pink sash.

Shows the "Laura" and "Robin" doll that apparently did not reach the retail shelves in 1981. The dolls are shown in six of the twelve outfits that were to be available for them. Taken from the 1981 Ideal catalog.

This 11½" "Loni Anderson" doll was shown in the 1981 Ideal catalog, but the doll never reached the market. The same body was to be used for 11½" "Laura" and "Robin" which were Black dolls, but these too were not released, or if any were put on the market they were in a very limited number. It must be noted that "Final sculpting of doll pending approval by Loni Anderson" is at the bottom of the page.

1982 was to see the introduction of the 3½″ "Angel Babies" which are delightful little creatures, but they did not reach the market. The panties are painted on and the waists are jointed and when half the doll is twisted they fluttered their wings. It is a shame that these dolls were not released. Available also was a Angel Baby pool with rainbow slide and pink diving board on a cloud like base and a multi-piece play house.

**Victorian Ladies** ™
**8″ & 12″ Costume Dolls**

"Victorian Ladies" in 8″ and 12″ sizes are shown in the 1983 Ideal catalog and their names are shown along side each doll. The 8″ was also used for the "Fairy Tale" Character Dolls and include: "Mother Goose," "Little Red Riding Hood," "Little Bo Peep," "Cinderella," "Snow White," and "Alice in Wonderland."

8″ "Little Southern Girl" made for the 3rd Annual Collector's United Down South Gathering and Show. 1983. All vinyl with rooted blonde hair, blue sleep eyes and slightly pouty mouth. Yellow ribbon tied in hair. Gown is yellow satin with white lace trim with yellow edging. Limited Edition of 600.

20″ "Shirley Temple." All composition and mint in the 1934 "Baby Take a Bow" pink pleated organdy dress that is tagged. Hair in original set and has original pin. Blue satin ribbon ties on skirt for arms and at waist and neck. (Courtesy Chester Wencel)

15″ "Shirley Temple" All composition and original and shown with unusual original trunk. The picture of Shirley with her finger at the side of her face is not a common one found on original doll trunks. (Courtesy Marge Meisinger)

20″ Flirty eyes with black eyeshadow "Shirley Temple" that is all original with pin. All composition doll. The jumper is royal blue, pleated pique′ with pink pique′ blouse and she has two white buttons at the shoulder straps. (Courtesy Ann Wencel)

18″ "Shirley Temple" that is all composition and shown in the white satin pajamas with red dots and buttons from "The Poor Little Rich Girl" movie. The outfit has the Shirley Temple tag at the waist. (Courtesy Martha Sweeney)

25″ "Shirley Temple." All composition and shown in all original "Heidi" tagged dress. The dress is red with white stars. She wears a white pinafore and has red bow in hair and at neck. (Courtesy Martha Sweeney)

27″ "Shirley Temple" in all original navy sailor suit with white trim on sleeves, red emblem and tie. Hair in original set. Has red buttons on pants. Outfit from the movie "Captain January." Has flirty eyes. Won blue ribbon at the Joliet show in 1982. (Courtesy Chester Wencel)

This shows the factory of the 1930's Cinderella Company that made the Shirley Temple children dresses. The building is still being used as a factory (not by the Cinderella firm) and is located in Pennsylvania. (Courtesy Kay Bransky)

19″ Shirley Temple that has a hard plastic body and is a walker. The vinyl head is different than the other dolls of 1950's. The hair is rooted and she has sleep eyes, open/closed mouth with four teeth. The arms are rigid vinyl and the doll is marked: IDEAL TOY CORP./G-18, on back and IDEAL TOY CORP/ST-19-8, on head. She is shown in original dotted swiss dress which is white with red dots, and with original name pin. (Courtesy Marge Meisinger)

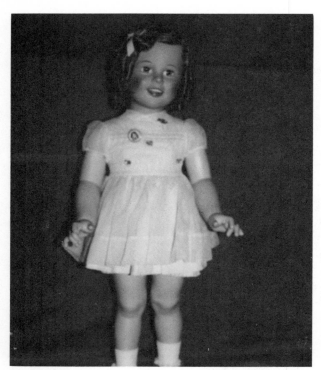

36″ "Shirley Temple" with plastic and vinyl body and head with rooted hair and wide smile. Hairdo is mint. Marks: IDEAL DOLL/ST 35-38-2, on head. (Courtesy Shirley Merrill)

This shows the flat box the Sara Stimson "Little Miss Marker" doll was marketed in. Picture window in front. (Courtesy Renie Culp)

11″ "Little Miss Marker" from the 1980 movie by the same name starring Sara Stimson. This was a re-make of a Shirley Temple movie of the 1930's. Dark brown painted eyes, dark brown rooted hair. Plastic body and legs with vinyl head and arms. Posable head. Marks: 1979/UNIV. STUDIOS/IDEAL, in oval/H-330/HONG KONG P, on head. IDEAL in oval/HONG KONG P, on back. (Courtesy Carol Friend)

8″ and 12″ 1982 "Shirley Temples" were available dressed as: "Stand Up and Cheer," "Heidi," "The Little Colonel," "The Littlest Rebel," "Captain January" and "Stowaway." Photo by the Ideal Toy Corp.

The 1983 Shirley Temples came in 8″ and 12″ sizes and their names are shown along side each doll. These are to be the last in the series of 12 dolls in each size over a two year period (1982 and 1983). Taken from the 1983 Ideal Catalog.

Left: 20″ All hard plastic walker with pin jointed hips. Arms and legs are strung, wig, sleep eyes, open mouth with tongue and four teeth. Marks: I.M.P.C.O. on head. Right: 22″ Hard plastic body and limbs with vinyl head rooted hair, sleep eyes and closed mouth. Jointed at knees. Marks: I.M.P. CO., on head. (Courtesy Jeannie Mauldin)

19″ Close up of an Imperial Crown walker that is all hard plastic. Has holes in chest for cryer. Sleep eyes, open mouth with tongue and four upper teeth. Light brown glued on wig. Marks: IMPCO, on head. (Courtesy Carol Friend)

5½″ Bent leg baby that is all rigid plastic with lamb's wool wig, painted eyes to side, open mouth/not a nurser. Finger pointing on right hand. Marks: MADE IN/IRWIN/USA, in circle on back. (Courtesy Virginia Jones)

7″ Bent leg baby that is all hard plastic with one piece body and head, painted black eyes and molded hair. Made by Irwin. (Courtesy Shirley Merrill)

2″ Hard plastic baby jointed at hips and shoulders and with one piece body and head. Painted features. Marks: IRWIN, on back. (Courtesy Shirley Merrill)

11″ All composition with blue eyes painted to side, mohair wig, rosebud style painted mouth. Original riding habit with white cotton blouse attached to tan riding pants, red vest of imitation leather, red grograin tie, brown imitation leather shoes, brown rayon socks. Blue cardboard pinned to vest. Made by Junel Dolls. (Courtesy Glorya Woods)

13″, 18″ and 21″ "Little Iodine" with vinyl head, deeply molded hair with large front curl to tie ribbon to, and one piece latex body and limbs. Made by the Juro Novelty Co. New York.

# From C.B.S. Coast to Coast Television
# The Beat The Clock "Rags to Riches" Doll

She changes in 4 quick steps from a poor little doll into a princess.

'TRADE MARK
PAT. PENDING

No. 1403 BEAT THE CLOCK
"RAGS TO RICHES" DOLL

From the C.B.S. Coast-to-coast T.V. show "Beat the Clock," this is the "Rags to Riches" doll. Came in 14″ and 20″ sizes. All vinyl with jointed waist. Came with two pairs of shoes, one gold and other black. "Rags" dress is pink with multi print ruffle, patches and kerchief, plus blue rickrack trim. This outfit is in two pieces. By removing blouse, untying the skirt and pushing it down, the dress becomes a gown of gold and red. Rooted hair, sleep eyes, has drop pearl earrings and double row pearl necklace. Also comes with gold crown. Made by the Juro Novelty Co. in 1957.

21″ "Lolita" All original and in original box. The doll has an adult figure, plastic body with vinyl head and limbs. Rooted hair and sleep eyes with heavy eyeshadow. Marked: KAYSAM.

17″ "Baby Won't Let Go." Plastic and vinyl, blue painted eyes, blonde rooted hair. Original clothes and hands curl around your fingers when the arms are lifted. Marks: 4046 TAIWAN K002 G.M.F.G.I. 1977 93, on head and G.M.F. G.I. 1977 KENNER PROD. DIV CIN'TI OHIO 45202 26150, on back. Can also be marked: TAIWAN K002/G.M.F.G.I. 1977/KENNER PROD. DIV. CIN'TI. OHIO 45202/28100 26150, on back and G.M.F.G.I. 1977/96, on head. (Courtesy Amy Merrill)

13″ "Oscar Goldman" Played by Richard Anderson. All plastic action figure with vinyl head. Blue torso. Molded hair and painted brown eyes. Marks: 1977 GENERAL MILLS FUN/GROUP INC. BY ITS DIVISION/KENNER PRODUCTS, CINCINNATI/OHIO 45202 CAT. NO. 65100/MADE IN HONG KONG/CHARACTER/UNIVERSAL CITY STUDIOS, INC. 1973/ALL RIGHTS RESERVED.

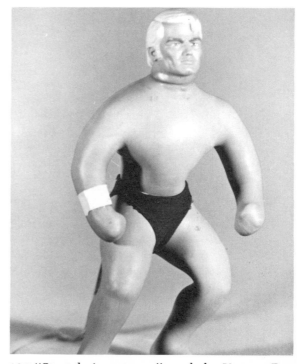

13″ "Stretch Armstrong" made by Kenner Products. Will stretch to over four feet and always returns to shape. Extremely heavy. Not marked. Molded blonde hair and has very good features on head. Jointed only at neck.

12″ "Shaun Cassidy" of T.V.'s Hardy Boys. Plastic body with vinyl arms and legs. Bendable knees. Vinyl head with molded hair and painted brown eyes. Open/closed mouth with painted teeth. Plastic guitar on which neck slides up to reveal a red de-coder lens. Hold to eye and can read invisible clue written by pencils that are included with doll. Marks: 1978 U.S.C.I., on head. G.M.F.G.I. 1978 KENNER PROD./CINCINNATI OHIO 45202/MADE IN HONG KONG, lower back.

12″ "Parker Stevenson" as Frank Hardy of the Hardy Boys T.V. program. Hard plastic body with vinyl head and limbs. Molded brown hair and painted blue eyes. Open/closed mouth with painted white area between lips. Bendable knees. No extra joints. Marks: GMFGI 1978 KENNER PROD./CINCINNATI OHIO 45202/MADE IN HONG KONG. Plastic back pack has "eye" to read secret messages. Pencils are included. Has head set.

13″ "Boba-Fett" from "The Empire Strikes Back." He is a galaxy Bounty Hunter. Full action figure with extra joints except at waist. All plastic painted gray and green with red on one arm, yellow on other with brown hands. The belt and green cape are removable. Has movable microphone type gadget attached to helmet and a see through "Bionic" style eye that magnifies. (Courtesy Ricky Paez)

15″ "Darth Vader" of "Star Wars." All black plastic with molded helmet and clothes. Removable cape. Jointed hips, shoulders and neck. Right hand molded to hold red light saber. Marks: GMFGI 1978/MADE IN HONG KONG. Made by Kenner Products. The Darth Vader voice was done by James Earl Jones. (Courtesy Ricky Paez)

185

11½″ "Princess Leia" (of Organa). Plastic body with jointed waist. Vinyl arms and legs (bendable). Excellent vinyl head with painted brown eyes. Open/closed mouth with painted teeth. Marks: G.M.I.F.G.I. 1978, on head. 1974 G.M.G.I. KENNER PROD./CINCINNATI OHIO 45202/US PAT. 33,862,512/MADE IN HONG KONG. Figure is from the movie "Star Wars." Part played by Carrie Fisher.

12″ "Luke Skywalker" of "Star Wars." Excellent quality hard plastic body with vinyl arms and legs (bendable), vinyl head with molded blonde hair. Painted blue eyes and open/closed mouth with painted teeth. Marks: G.M.F.G.I. 1978, head. G.M.F.G.I. 1978 KENNER PROD./Cincinnati Ohio 45202/MADE IN HONG KONG, on back. Played by Mark Hamill.

11½″ "International Velvet". Sarah Velvet Brown, played by Tatum O'Neill. Plastic body with jointed waist. Vinyl arms and legs. Legs are bendable at knees. Flat feet with holes in heels. (also in bottom of boots) Marks 43/HONG KONG/1976 U.S.C.I., on head. 1978 G.M.F.G.I. KENNER PROD./CINCINNATI OHIO 45202/MADE IN HONG KONG, on lower back. Blue painted eyes and open/closed mouth with painted teeth. Also available is horse "Arizona-Pie." Box is marked: METRO-GOLDWYN MEYER.

12½″ "Darcie Cover Girl" dressed in one of her original outfits called "Garden Party." Marks: 140 HON KONG/GMFGI 1978. Made by Kenner. All vinyl and very posable and with painted features. (Courtesy Renie Culp)

12½″ "Darci Cover Girl" that is all vinyl and has painted features. Shown in original box. She came in several hair colors and dress styles and had many outfits available for her. Made in 1978 by Kenner.

12¼″ "Erica," "Darcie's" best friend. Uses same body. "Erica" has red hair and painted features and has a gold colored mask included in box. Marks: G.M.F.G.I. 1978, on head. C.R.G. PRODUCTS CORP. 1978/KENNER CINCINNATI/47400 MADE IN HONG KONG, on lower back. (Courtesy Renie Culp)

12½″ Black Cover Girl "Dana" with same body as the "Erica" and "Darci" dolls. Marks: 56 HONG KONG/G.M.F.G.I. 1978, on head. (Courtesy Renie Culp)

9″ "Sour Grapes" and her pet purple snake "Dregs" of the Strawberry Shortcake Collection. Blue and purple rooted hair, painted features with purple brows. Vinyl head with rigid plastic body and limbs. All purple legs with molded on boots and has green molded on long gloves. Purple dress with grapes printed on, grape earrings and doll smells like grapes. Marks: AMERICAN GREETING CORP. 1982, on head. A.G.C./1982, on snake. Box: KENNER.

11″ "Kuddles" by Knickerbocker Toy Co. Stuffed corduroy with vinyl head and hands. Deeply molded brown hair, black eyes painted to the side. Left hand thumb and two fingers are molded together, right has 3rd finger curled into the palm. Marks: KNICKERBOCKER/1965, on head. (Courtesy Jayn Allen)

16″ Double headed "Cinderella" with one side as "Poor Cinderella" and other in ball gown and with molded crown on head. The dolls are vinyl and jointed only at the shoulders. "Poor Cinderella" has hair pulled to top of head and has tear molded on corner of one eye. Made by Knickerbocker Toys in 1960's.

5½″ "Betsy Clark" with moveable vinyl head with rooted hair and painted features. Vinyl body and limbs, original clothes and accessories. Marks: KTC/HONG KONG. (Courtesy Mrs. Frank Miller)

11″ "Gnome" with vinyl head, painted features, cloth body and legs. Blue and brown outfit with orange hat. Taken from book of "Gnomes." Tag: KNICKERBOCKER 1978 UNIEBOLK B.V. Doll has white hair and bear. (Courtesy Mary Wheatley)

12″ "Laura" (left) and "Carrie" (right) from the TV series "Little House on the Prairie." Vinyl heads and hands, cloth bodies and legs. Name printed on pockets and dress tagged: LITTLE HOUSE ON THE PRAIRIE. Made by Knickerbocker Toy Corp. Heads are marked: 1978 ED FRIENDLY PRODUCTIONS, INC./LIC JLM/MADE IN TAIWAN T-2 (Courtesy Renie Culp)

6″ Official "Seattle Seahawk" doll. Cute all vinyl doll with rooted hair and painted eyes. Marks: NFL PROTERTIES, INC. (mis-spelled)/1976 K.T.C./MADE IN TAIWAN/T33. Football has NFL on it. And the head is marked: 1976 NFL PROPERTIES, INC. Sold through Montgomery Wards Christmas 1976. There was one representing each team. Made by Knickerbocker. (Courtesy Renie Culp)

6″ "Annie" representing Aileen Quinn from the 1982 movie "Annie." Plastic body with rigid vinyl limbs and vinyl head with rooted hair, painted features. Head is unmarked. Body mark is sidewards: 1982 CPI INC. 1982 CTNYNS, INC/1982 KNICKERBOCKER TOY CO. INC. H-15. Orange hair, freckles, red dress with white trim and blue stitching, white socks and blue shoes.

7″ "Daddy Warbucks" from the movie "Annie" played by Albert Finney. Marks are same as "Annie" sidewards down the back except the last is: "H-22." Plastic body with rigid vinyl legs and arms and bold vinyl head. Painted features. Dressed in black tux with red cummerbund and white shirt with black tie.

7″ "Miss Hannigan" from the movie "Annie" and played by Carol Burnett. Plastic body with rigid vinyl limbs and vinyl head with rooted brown hair, painted features and high heel feet. Dressed in purple with multi-color dots and ruffles. Purple shoes. Marks are the same as the "Daddy Warbucks" and "Punjab."

7″ "Punjab" from the movie "Annie" and played by Geoffrey Holder. Doll made the same and marked the same as the "Daddy Warbucks," except has dark skin tones. Black features and molded, painted hair under turbin. Dressed in white with red and gold accents.

5¾″ "Molly" from the movie "Annie" and played by Toni Ann Gisondi. Plastic body, rigid vinyl limbs and vinyl head with rooted long brown hair with full bangs. Painted features and marked same as others except number is "H-17." Dressed in aqua dress with floral sleeves and collar and has three patchs on dress. White leotards and brown shoes. The painted eyes are also brown. She also has a pair of plastic pink slippers in the box.

14" "Buddy Lee." All hard plastic with one piece body, legs and head. Painted features and in original Lee Engineer coveralls. Painted on black shoes. Original cap says: SEABORD RAILROAD, around the outside and THROUGH/THE HEART/OF THE /SOUTH in a heart in center of patch. The Seabord Railroad merged with the Coastline Railroad several years ago. (Courtesy Eloise Godfrey)

11" All Lastic-Plastic. Doll is made completely in one piece and is fully stuffed. Black wig is glued on and she has inset purple eyes. Owner also has a blonde with pink eyes. Original Strapless dress, replaced shoes. All fingers on right hand molded together, and fingers of left hand have 2nd and 3rd fingers molded together. (Courtesy Virginia Dean)

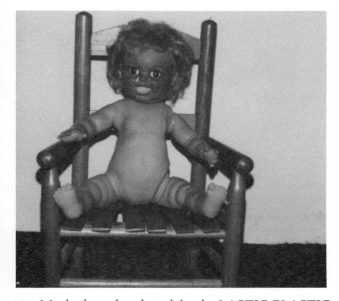

22" Marked on head and back: LASTIC-PLASTIC 1951. Stuffed vinyl, rooted hair done by hand, large brown eyes, open/closed smiling mouth with molded tongue. Dimples in cheeks. The inside edge of legs and ears marked: COPYRIGHT 1950 LASTIC-PLASTIC, She has turned dark due to early material. (Courtesy Jeannie Mauldin)

16" "Angel." Stuffed vinyl with molded blonde hair, closed eyes and came dressed as Angel praying. Made of Lastic-Plastic. 1950's. Unmarked. (Courtesy Mary Wheatley)

20″ "I Dream of Jeannie" from T.V. series by same name played by Barbara Eden. Plastic and vinyl with rooted hair and sleep eyes. Left is dressed in green with white trim and paisly print pants with white shoes. Right is all deep rose with white trim. Made by Libby. Marks: 4/1966/LIBBY, on head. (Courtesy Ann Wencel)

8″ "Phantom of the Opera" on left. Marks: LINCOLN/1976, on head. Fully jointed including waist, elbows, wrists, knees and ankles. Head is purple with very wide open/closed mouth. Right is 8″ "Hunchback of Notre Dame" with same description as the "Phantom."

20″ Composition shoulder plate and lower arms. Cloth body with cryer. Dark brown celluloid sleep eyes. Brown mohair over molded hair, open crown. Cloak not original. May be Madame Hendron. Ca. 1924. (Courtesy Nancy Lucas)

22″ "Baby Ruth" with composition head, deep shoulderplate, and lower arms. Painted blue eyes, brown mohair wig, doll is unmarked but shown in 1917 catalogs. Clothes not original. (Courtesy Nancy Lucas)

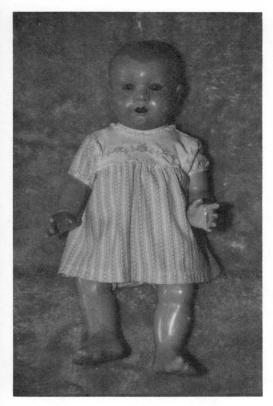

23″ All composition, fully jointed. Molded hair, green sleep eyes, green eyeshadow. Open mouth with felt tongue and two upper teeth. Not original. Marks: C in circle, something unreadable, JOHNSON MFG. (Courtesy Shirley Merrill)

22″ "Dolly Sunshine" made for Sears in 1929. Doll unmarked. Composition shoulder plate head, arms, and legs. Cloth body. Dimples, open mouth with felt tongue and two teeth, blonde mohair wig over molded hair, blue tin sleep eyes. Original, but had bonnet. (Courtesy Nancy Lucas)

16″ All composition Shirley Temple look-a-like. Human hair brown wig, brown tin sleep eyes, open mouth with teeth, felt tongue, dimples and original gown. (Courtesy Kay Bransky)

12″ Unmarked all composition dolls with painted features, molded painted hair and all original clothes. He has mohair mustache. (Courtesy Sally Bethscheider)

12″ All composition with one piece body and head, painted blue eyes and glued on blonde wig. Original clothes except shoes and socks. (Courtesy Betty Wood)

17″ All composition, blue sleep eyes, brown human hair wig, original clothes, replaced shoes. 2nd and 3rd fingers molded together and slightly curled. Unmarked. (Courtesy Shirley Merrill)

8″ Bridal Party with "Bride," "Groom" and four "Bridesmaids." All composition with two having blue painted eyes and the rest have brown painted eyes. The "Groom" has molded hair and rest have mohair wigs. "Bride" is not original, but rest are. The "Bridesmaids" are dressed in pink and blue, and in green and peach. All the dolls are unmarked and could have been made by Joy, Junel or Mollye Goldman. (Courtesy Marge Meisinger)

14″ "Scrappy" with cloth body, arms and legs. Composition head with painted hair and features, composition very large hands and feet. White shirt with red short pants with shoulder straps. A Columbia Pictures and Winkler Film Corp. Cartoon Character. Ca. 1934. The Big-Little book dated 1934. (Courtesy Ruth Rivasi)

9″ "Rabbit" tightly stuffed pink mohair (also came in blue) that is very well defined and made. Composition head with blue painted eyes and molded hair. Wire runs through ears and into head so bonnet is not removable. Umarked. Ca. 1930. (Courtesy Kathy Feagans)

19″ "Abbi-Gail." All composition with wide open/closed mouth. Sleep brown eyes and original caracul wig. Deep red stripe jumper skirt. Same material with white top one piece panties/top. Distinctive hand modelling. Not marked, but very much like Horsman dolls. 1948.

19″ "Abbi-Gail" All composition with mohair wig, blue sleep eyes. Not original. 1948. Hands are modeled just like many composition dolls by Horsman. (Courtesy Shirley Merrill)

14″ Composition that is all original with "fur" hat, white silk outfit trimmed with gold rick rack and gold underlining. Wood baton. Mohair wig, painted features and very rosy composition. (Courtesy Kay Bransky)

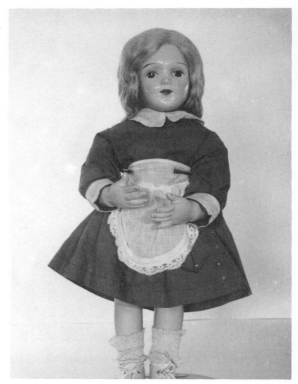

19″ Composition head, legs and arms, oversized hands. Blue uniform is original with white collar and apron. Blonde mohair wig, cloth body, blue painted eyes. (Courtesy Kay Bransky)

10″ "Cowboy." Head and hands are leather. Back of doll is flat piece of felt. Shirt is green silk and kerchief is yellow silk. Lambswool chaps. No marks. Maker and date are unknown. Painted features and hair. (Courtesy Peg Webber) (Photo by Sally Freeman)

20″ Unmarked Kewpie-type with flannel cloth body and limbs, composition head with molded, painted hair at top and sides, painted features and watermelon smile. (Courtesy Shirley Merrill)

8″ "Millie." All hard plastic walker, head turns. Sleep eyes/molded lashes. Glued on wig. No marks on doll or box.

10″ All hard plastic, fully jointed, blue sleep eyes, molded hair, open/closed mouth. Good modeling and quality. Unmarked. Looks like a "Tiny Tears" or "Dy Dee" of the early 1950's. Not original clothes. (Courtesy Shirley Merrill)

26″ Unmarked. Very much like the large size Alexanders, and something like the "Girls of Tomorrow." Has rooted hair that is plugged individually and not by machine. Cloth body with early stuffed vinyl limbs and head, large sleep eyes/lashes and molded lids. Individual fingers and excellent modeling. Long slender limbs. May be original clothes.

 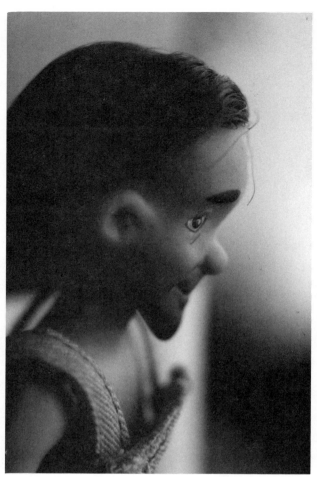

9″ Character doll that looks like a personality. All vinyl body and limbs, jointed at neck, shoulder and hips, original overalls. Pointed chin painted to look like a beard, painted blue eyes, heavy brows and side part rooted hair that is brown. (Courtesy Sheryl Schmidt)

14″ Unmarked, in original maid uniform. Plastic and vinyl with rooted hair in braids, inset blue eyes and open/closed mouth. (Courtesy Jewel Smith)

16″ Eskimo Child. Brown rigid plastic with well modeled arms, thinner plastic torso and legs, rooted hair and has inset brown eyes with painted irises, two stroke eyebrows, pug nose and original cotton flannel snowsuit with synthetic fur trim. Ca. 1950's. (Courtesy Margaret Mandel)

12″ Unmarked latex vinyl one piece body with vinyl head "Hansel." Deeply molded hair, and painted blue eyes to the side. Open/closed mouth with molded tongue. Looks very much like a Baby Hungerford. (Courtesy Jayn Allen)

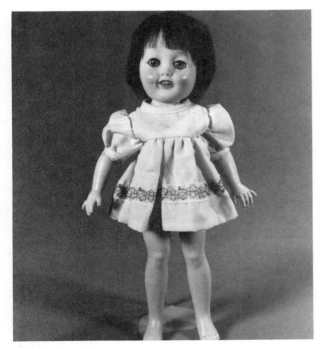

13¼″ Shirley Temple look-a-like. All excellent quality vinyl with sleep blue eyes/lashes. Open mouth with four teeth and dimples. Marks: 13S. Can't tell original hair style, as hair has most likely been cut. Not original dress. The quality of the vinyl and modeling looks very much like Ideal Toy Company's workmanship of the late 1950's, early 1960's. (Courtesy Jayn Allen)

12″ Left: is "Dr. Kildare," played on TV by Richard Chamberlin with molded hair and painted features. Right: "Dr. Ben Casey" played by Vince Edwards. Both are all original with names printed on pockets, along with the medical emblem. Both dolls have rather poor quality bodies, but the heads have rather good modeling. Jointed at neck, shoulders and hips and both are unmarked. Ca. 1963. (Courtesy Nancy Lucas)

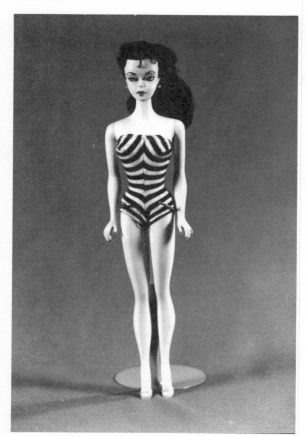

Full length view of #1 "Barbie." Has inverted "V" eyebrows, white irises, not blue, in eyes and has holes in bottom of feet to go on metal black round stand with two metal prongs. Bright red lips and nails, black and white stripe bathing suit and gold hoope earrings. The #2 Barbie is basically the same as #1 only does not have the holes in bottom of feet. Marks: BARBIE/PATS. PEND/MCMLVIII/BY/MATTEL/INC.

The box that the #1 Barbie came in.

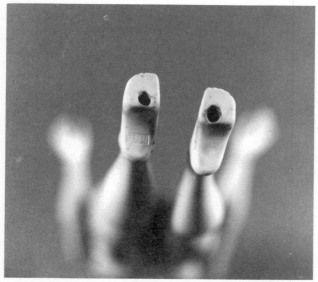

This shows the holes in the bottom of the #1 Barbie's feet. There are metal cylinders inside the holes. Also shows the "Japan" stamp that is on the bottom of many of the Barbie feet.

The #1 booklet that came in the first boxes only had Barbie by herself on the cover.

16½″ long blue and red car with chrome engine. White interior and red roll bar. Made by Irwin for "Barbie." Irwin also made the 1963 Sports car for "Barbie." These street rods had lost favor to the public and the sports cars (Corvettes) were the most desirable cars, thus this hot rod will be a harder item to find than the sports car. Made in 1963.

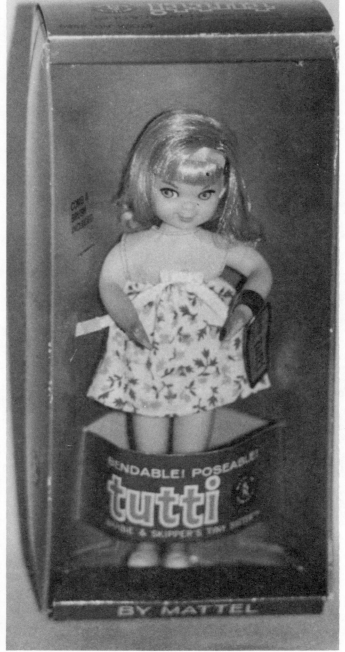

6″ "Tutti." Left: pink check "playsuit" and hat #3550 and right: #3603 "Sand Castles" white with red dots hat and playsuit. 1965. (Courtesy Linda Crowsey)

6″ "Tutti" with one piece, bendable body and limbs. Rooted hair and painted eyes. Mint in box #3580 wearing a print pink skirt with solid pink top. 1965. (Courtesy Linda Crowsey)

6″ "Tutti." Right: blue check top with red trim and red leotards and tagged: TUTTI. Left: White nylon long gown with blue embroidery trim. 1966. (Courtesy Linda Crowsey)

11½″ "Beauty Secrets Barbie" Original. #1296 and marked: MATTEL, INC. 1979 TAIWAN 1966. Push button in back to move arms. (Courtesy Mrs. Frank Miller)

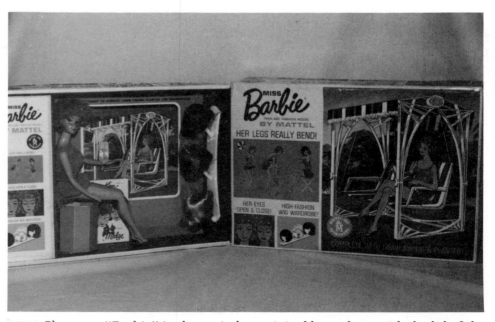

11½″ Sleep eye "Barbie" is shown in her original box, along with the lid of the box. Eyes are cut up at an angle, she has molded hair and bend knees. Came with three wigs, pink cap and lawn swing and planter. Made in 1964. (Courtesy Pat Timmons)

11½″ "Ballerina Barbie" Original. Marks: MAT-TEL, INC. 1966/U.S. PAT. PENDING. TAIWAN. Available in 1979. (Courtesy Mrs. Frank Miller)

11½″ "Pretty Changes" Barbie. Original clothes. Marks: MATTEL INC. 1966/PHILLIPINES. Available in 1979. (Courtesy Mrs. Frank Miller)

11½″ "Superstar Barbie." Arms are molded bent at elbows. Gown is rose-red sequined and hair piece is silver sequined. Painted blue eyes. Open/closed mouth with painted teeth. (Courtesy Renie Culp)

11½″ "Superstar Barbie Bride" #9907. Ring is on the right hand. (Courtesy Renie Culp)

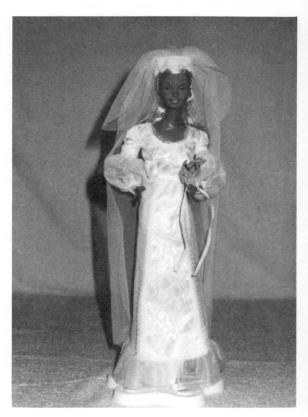

18″ "Super Size Barbie" that is called "Christie." Black version of "Barbie." Orangish rooted hair. Painted brown eyes. Arms molded bent at elbows. Gown is blue with silver inset panel. (Courtesy Renie Culp)

18″ "Super Size Barbie" shown in wedding gown #9975, which was sold separately. (Courtesy Renie Culp)

11½″ "Hawaiian Barbie" that is marked what looks like "KOK23" right at hairline, and MATTEL, INC./1966 KOREA, on backside. Black long straight rooted hair, tan skin tones, came this outfit with variations to print, has plastic lei and "Hobie" style surfer with white base and red sail. (Courtesy Renie Culp)

11½″ "Royal Barbie-England" Marks: MATTEL, INC. 1966/TAIWAN, on back waist. Gown is white with red banner across on shoulder, both arms are bent and non-posable, holds gold wand, has back band in blonde hair. (Courtesy Renie Culp)

11½" "Hispanic Barbie" #1292-,980. Marks: MATTEL 1966/TAIWAN, on back waist. Non-posable bent plastic arms and in original white, red and black clothes. 1982. (Courtesy Renie Culp)

12" "Gold Medal Big Jack" 1974. Press cut out in back to make right arm move. Marks: 1971 MATTEL, INC./HONG KONG, U.S. &/FOREIGN PATENTED. Torso is painted white with red and blue stars and bands to resemble bathing suit.

9½" "Super Teen Skipper" Marks: MATTEL, INC. 1978/MATTEL 1967/Phillipines. (Courtesy Mrs. Frank Miller)

10" "Scott"-Skipper's boyfriend. #1019. Marks: 2200-2109/MATTEL INC. 1968/PHILLIPINES. Also had denim & yellow jacket. (Courtesy Mrs. Frank Miller)

10" "Grizzly Adams." Plastic body with red lower torso. Full action figure with vinyl arms. Cut out mechanism in back to make right arm move. Vinyl head with molded hair and beard. Painted brown eyes. Open/closed mouth with painted teeth. "Big Jim" body. Marks: 1971 MATTEL INC./US & FOREIGN PATENTS/HONG KONG, on back.

10" "Zeb Macahan" from "How the West Was Won" T.V. show. Molded blonde hair and mustache. Painted blue eyes. Full action figure. Marks: same as "Lone Wolf." Played by James Arness.

9½" "Lone Wolf" from T.V. series "How The West Was Won." Plastic body and legs, cut out mechanism in back to operate arm. White lower torso. Vinyl arms and head, plastic hands. Rooted hair and painted black eyes. Marks: 1975 MATTEL INC, on head with HONG KONG sidewards. 1971 MATTEL INC/HONG KONG U.S. &/FOREIGN PATENTED, on lower back.

10" "Warpath." Full action figure with white torso. Vinyl oversleeve arms with mechanism in back to operate arm. Has wolf head stamped on left hand. Marks: 1971 MATTEL INC./U.S. & FOREIGN PATENTED/HONG KONG. Made in 1975.

10" "The Whip." Weapon's Specialist. Full action figure with white torso. Mechanism in back to operate arm. Wolf head stamped on hand. Molded black hair, brows, mustache and beard. Marks: 1971 MATTEL INC/HONG KONG U.S. &/FOREIGN PATENTED. 1975. Part of Big Jim P.A.C.K.(Professional Agents/Crime Killers). Other members are "Dr. Steel" and "Warpath."

12" "Shaun" #1283. Marks: MATTEL, INC. 1979, on head and MATTEL INC. 1975/Taiwan, across waist. Has extra joints at wrists and holds plastic guitar. Blonde molded hair, painted blue eyes and open/closed smiling mouth. Dressed in original jeans, multi stripe shirt and deep rose satin jacket with white trim. (Courtesy Renie Culp)

11½" "Debbie Boone" Marks: RESI. INC. 1978 TAIWAN, on head and MATTEL, INC. 1966/TAIWAN, on back. All original. Has one piece molded bent arms, microphone in one hand and an open/closed smiling mouth. (Courtesy Renie Culp)

12" "Kitty O'Neill." Green painted eyes. Open/closed mouth with painted teeth, using Barbie body. Plastic body and arms. Jointed at waist. Vinyl legs with bendable knees. Name on jumpsuit and belt. Marks: MATTEL INC. 1966, on upper back. Head isn't marked. T.V. star daredevil stuntwoman.

11½" "Marie Osmond." Vinyl head, rooted brown hair. Brown painted eyes, open/closed mouth, painted teeth. Rigid vinyl arms with microphone "plugged" into right hand. Vinyl legs, bendable knees. Skating outfit was one of the extra outfits sold for the doll. Marks: MATTEL INC./1966/12 KOREA, on body. Uses old Barbie body. "Donny & Marie Osmond" were also marketed as 11½" puppets in 1978 through Montgomery Wards.

30" "Marie Osmond." Plastic one piece torso and legs. Jointed waist with plastic upper body. Vinyl arms and head. Molded on panties and bra. Medium high heel feet. Comes with a package of patterns for making clothes. Marks: OSBRO PROD. 1975, on head. Same on body, plus has U.S.A. sideward on upper neck.

10" "Jimmy Osmond" Plastic body, rigid vinyl arms and legs (knees do not bend), molded hair, painted brown eyes, freckles and open/closed smiling mouth. Left arm molded bent at elbow with hole in hand to attach mike. Marks: 22---2109/MATTEL INC./1966/TAIWAN, on lower back. On market in 1979.

11¾" "Donny Osmond." Vinyl head and bendable legs. Plastic body and arms with microphone attached to left hand. Molded brown hair, painted brown eyes. Open/closed mouth with painted teeth. Marks: 10-88-05005/MATTEL/INC. 1968/HONG KONG.

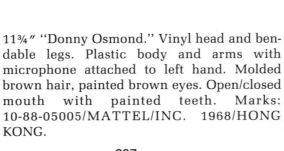

11½″ "Starr" #1280. Marks: MATTEL, INC. 1979, on head and MATTEL, INC. 1979/PHILIPINES, on back. Bendable knees, arms, jointed at wrists. Blonde rooted hair and original Math book. Painted features. (Courtesy Renie Culp)

11½″ "Kelly" #1281. With marks and description same as "Starr," only has red rooted hair with green head band and carries History book. (Courtesy Renie Culp)

11½″ "Tracy" #1282. Marks and description same as "Starr" but has brunette rooted hair, is on skates and carries Art book. (Courtesy Renie Culp)

Left: 9½″ "Kristy McNichols" made by Mego and marked: MEGO CORP. MADE IN HONG KONG, on head and 1977 MEGO CORP./MADE IN HONG KONG, on back. Right: 9¼″ "Buddy"-"Kristy McNichols" from the T.V. show "Family" Marks: 1978 SPELLING GOLDBERG PROD., on head. MATTEL INC. 1978, on back top part of waist and MATTEL INC. 1967, on lower part of back at waist. She has "Buddy" on shirt and a "B" on jacket. She also came boxed with extra skirt. (Courtesy Renie Culp)

11½″ "Cheryl Ladd" of Charlie's Angels. Packaged as "T.V.'s Star Women." Plastic body with rigid vinyl arms. Vinyl legs with bendable knees, vinyl head, painted eyes that are green. open/closed mouth with painted teeth. Rooted hair. Jointed waist. Marks: MATTEL 1966/KOREA and a "13" to the left. Uses old Barbie body.

11½″ "Kate Jackson" of Charlie's Angels. Same body description as Cheryl Ladd, but had brown painted eyes and rooted brown hair. Marks: MATTEL, INC/1978 head. MATTEL INC./1966/Korea, and a "13" to the left, on lower back.

"Barbarino" and "Epstein" from the "Welcome Back, Kotter" television program. Marks: WOLPER-KOMACK, on head. 1973/MATTEL INC/TAIWAN, on lower backs. "Barbarino" played by John Travolta "Epstein" played by Robert Hegyes.

"Washington" and "Horshack" from "Welcome Back Kotter" Marks: WOLPER-KOMACK, on heads. 1973/MATTEL INC./TAIWAN, on lower backs. "Washington" played by Lawrence Hilton Jacobs and "Horshack" by Ron Palillo.

"Mr. Kotter" from the T.V. program, "Welcome Back, Kotter." Marks: WOLPER-KOMACK, on head. 1973/MATTEL INC/TAIWAN, on lower back. Played by Gabriel Kaplan.

9″ "Mork" and 8½″ "Mindy." Marks on Mork: Wrist tag: TAIWAN, 1979 P.P.C. TAIWAN, on head and 1973 MATTEL INC. TAIWAN, on body. Mindy's marks: 1979 P.P.C. TAIWAN, on head and 1973 MATTEL INC. TAIWAN, on back. He has molded hair, painted features and came with back pack, says eight phrases. She has rooted hair, open/closed mouth and painted eyes to sides. Both original. (Courtesy Renie Culp)

4″ "Mork from Ork" that is all rigid vinyl, fully jointed and has molded on clothes. Molded hair and egg is marked: MORK FROM ORK. Made by Mattel. (Courtesy Renie Culp)

18″ "Sister Belle" of 1961. Dolls have eyes painted to sides with one looking to left and other to the right. The doll on left also as a smaller mouth. Both are marked MATTEL, INC. HAWTHORNE, on head and have body tags: MATTEL, INC. Both are original. (Courtesy Jeannie Mauldin)

25″ "Charmin' Chatty" Marks: Charmin' Chatty 1961 Mattel. Dressed in "Lets Play Cinderella" #362 that has a ballgown of metallic net over taffeta, cape and "Glass" slippers, plus wand. Also comes with tattered dress and mop. Pull-ring talker with records. This record plays, "Cinderella Goes To The Ball." (Courtesy Ann Wencel)

15″ "Pedal Pretty." All original cloth doll with face mask, yarn hair, painted features, freckles. Has tricycle, wagon with velcro on peddles and seat so doll can ride. Tag: MATTEL PEDAL PRETTY 1973 MATTEL INC., HAWTHORNE, CALIF. 90250. (Courtesy Jeannie Mauldin)

4″ "Baby White Star Rose." The gown is white with two rows of lace down front, rosette and ribbon. Her hair is blonde, eyes are blue and she comes with cradle covered in pale pink, also a rocker and night stand.

4″ "Lavender Lace Rose" that comes with a stroller with pink satin cushion seat and pink covered. Her hair is blonde and she has painted blue eyes. The gown is pale lavender with darker satin lavender underneath. Marks: MATTEL, INC. 1976/Taiwan.

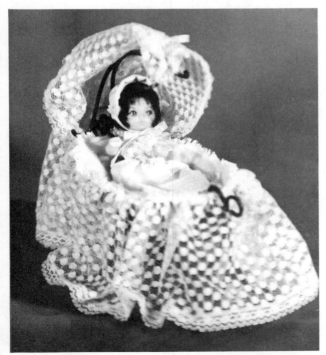

4″ "Pink Heather Rose" comes in cradle covered with white. She has brown hair, brown painted eyes and her gown is dotted pink with rosette in front. marks: MATTEL, INC. 1976/TAIWAN.

4″ "Baby Darling Rose." Blonde with either blue or green eyes. Peach colored gown under sheer white. Good quality vinyl/rigid plastic. Marks: MATTEL INC. 1976/TAIWAN.

7½″ "Marissa Rosebud." Vinyl head and plastic body and limbs. Original clothes, rooted hair and painted eyes. The hair is red. Marks: MATTEL INC. 1976/TAIWAN. (Courtesy Mrs. Frank Miller)

7½″ "Silvie Rosebud." Brunette with painted eyes, rooted hair, plastic body and limbs, and vinyl head. Marks: MATTEL, INC. 1976/TAIWAN. (Courtesy Mrs. Frank Miller)

4″ "Scarlet Gem Rose." Deep rose under sheer white gown. Rooted hair is red and painted eyes are blue. Marks: MATTEL, INC. 1976/TAIWAN.

4″ "Baby Gold Star Rose." Brown rooted hair and brown painted eyes. Yellow gown. Marks: MATTEL, INC. 1976/TAIWAN.

7½" "Gorgeous Creatures." All are marked: MATTEL, INC. 1979/PHILIPPINES. Top left: "Ms. Giddie Yup" in hot pink and silver with blonde hair. Undressed so the body can be seen. The bodies are very, very, "Mae West"-like with molded on undies. Top right: "Princess Pig" in lavender and black. Lower left: "Cow Belle" in blue/lavender and "Ms. Heavenly Hippo" in yellow with red hair.

15" "Love 'n Touch Real Sister" with vinyl head and hands with rest cloth. Blue painted eyes, on blonde. Brown painted eyes on Black version. Rooted hair. Original. Marks: MATTEL INC. 1980 TAIWAN, on head. (Courtesy Carol Friend)

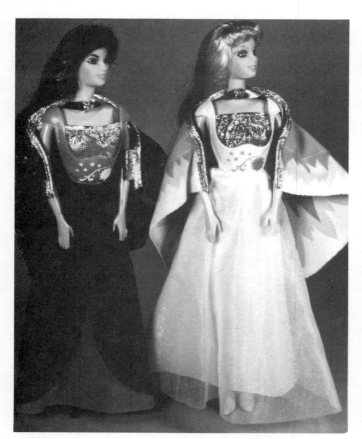

Mattel made the "Guardian Goddesses" in 1979/1980. Some were put in test play rooms and in test stores. They are really fantastic Barbie-style (size and adult figures) dolls, but it was found that children could break them after a few hours of play, so they were not produced for the mass market. Anyone having them are fortunate, as they are very high priced collector's items and will go much higher as time goes by. Left: "Moonmystic" and right is "Sunspell" with arms down and gowns on. When the dolls legs are pulled apart the arms fly up and the dresses pop off to reveal the underneath outfits.

Only four extra outfits were available for these dolls:
Left: "Lion Queen" and right is "Ice Empress"

Left: "Blazing Fire" and right is "Soaring Eagle." All
these outfits are especially pretty, but there are so
many pieces that children found them hard to manage.
(Author)

1981-1982 Japanese "Barbie." Has vinyl
limbs that are posable like the "Tutti" and
"Todd" dolls. Very large painted eyes,
rooted hair and marked: MATTEL INC.
JAPAN. (Taken from brochure, Courtesy
Margaret Mandel)

Shows some of the clothes available for the Japanese "Barbie."
(Courtesy Margaret Mandel)

# Mattel's Collector Dolls

During 1982 Mattel introduced two groups of "Collector" dolls: La Cheri and Sala & Berg, and they were limited to 1200 dolls each with every doll wearing a cork tag on the wrist bearing the serial number and year.

In 1983 Mattel introduced the second series of these sets of "Collector" dolls with the Sala & Berg being limited to 2000 each and the limited number for the La Cheri dolls at 1800 each. The 1983 dolls have a leather tag with the serial number and year at the wrist.

1983 also saw Mattel bring out a series called "Magic of Mariko." The four dolls have a unique contemporary look, limited to 1800 of each doll and wear a triangular leather tag showing the year of introduction and the number.

All of Mattel "Collector" dolls are made by Sekiguchi in Japan and Mattel is the exclusive distributor of Sekiguchi dolls in the United States.

Shown are the collector's Classic Beauty Collection of 1977 and 1978. Plastic and vinyl with rooted hair, sleep eyes. Dolls are excellent quality as are the clothes. Upper left: "Cecelia" and right: Cassandra." Lower left: "Catherine" and right is Cynthia." Mattel furnished production totals on the dolls and they are: Cecelia-3,005; Cassandra-2,761; Catherine-2,799 and Cynthia-3,731.

#1000 Parisian BARBIE Doll

These are "Department Store" specials made by Mattel in 1982 and 1983. Top: "Parisian" in pink and black, "Scottish" in red and black. Bottom: "Oriental" with darker skin tones and differently painted eyes dressed in gold and red and new for 1983 was "Swedish" in blue, white and black with red trim. Mattel catalog. 1983.

Special production "Department Store" Barbies. Top is Eskimo and right is India, both also available in 1982. New for 1983 is the change of clothes on the Spanish Barbie. All have dark skin tones and the India has very large, expressive eyes.

#3898
Eskimo BARBIE Doll

NEW '83

#4031 Spanish BARBIE Doll

#3897 India BARBIE Doll

LA CHERI French Country Garden Collection

#5531 LA CHERI doll in burgundy

#5530 LA CHERI doll in blue

#5529 LA CHERI doll in p

18″ "La Cheri" collection for 1982, limited to 1800 of each doll. They are also called the "French Country Garden Collection." All are 18″ tall, have European dark skin tones, blonde hair and dark brown eyes. Standing: in Burgandy with matching burgandy straw hat, burgandy floral print pinafore. White yoke, sleeve edges and a burgandy velvet ribbon at neck. Left: Same, only in blues and right: same only in pink. Tagged with serial number and date. Made in Japan by Sekiguchi, for Mattel.

**MATTEL**

## MATTEL COLLECTOR DOLLS

# sala & berg

### Limited Edition Series II

The magic of an Alpine fairy tale is captured in the Sala & Berg Series II. These handsome 14" dolls are the second pair in this limited edition series. Strikingly European looking, each doll is dressed in authentically designed clothing. Even their shoes are finely crafted. Sala wears a pretty pinafore with lace detail over a plaid dress, a bell around her neck, and elaborate undergarments. Berg is dressed in a plaid shirt, brown vest, corduroy trousers, cap, "sheepskin" bag and horn. Innocent, childlike features, beautiful brown eyes and a generous amount of gorgeous hair make these dolls irresistibly special to collectors. Each Sala & Berg doll is tagged with a distinctive leather tag bearing a serial number and the year in order to insure its collectibility as a limited edition doll. The designer package is of exceptional quality, with the Sala & Berg logo richly displayed in gold lettering.

**#4722 Asst. Pak 4**
**#4720 Std. Pak 2**
**#4721 Std. Pak 2**

#4720 BERG boy doll

#4721 SALA girl doll

SALA & BERG Series II

14" "Sala & Berg" dolls of 1983 and limited to 2000 of each doll. The 1983 dolls represent Alpine fairy tales. The boy is dressed in green/tan wool shirt, tan corduroy pants, brown cap and vest, carries a "sheepskin" bag and a plastic horn. The girl is in plaid dress with pink pinafore apron and carries a bell. They both have a leather tag stating date and number. Mattel has these dolls made by Sekiguchi of Japan. The 1982 set had boy dressed in brown pants, plaid shirt and green knit sweater and matching green knit cap. The girl was in blue plaid, burgandy sweater and cap with white collar and sleeve edges. They had a wooden tag at wrist with the name Sala & Berg, date and number. The 1982 dolls were limited to 1200 each.

220

MATTEL COLLECTOR DOLLS

# La Cheri
## Limited Edition Series II

Say "Bonjour" to La Cheri—three lovely mademoiselles from the French Country Garden Collection. Each 18" doll has warm European coloring and beautifully sculpted face and hands. Her hair is thick and flowing, and her big brown eyes are warm and sparkling. Dressed in a burgundy coat, matching French cap, petticoat-type dress and black stockings, the oldest sister is off to visit Grandmama. Her two sisters stay home and pick flowers from Papa's garden. One wears a pink pinafore with matching print dress and straw hat. The other, a white pinafore with navy blue print dress and straw hat. Personalized attention has been given to their authentically designed clothes, including beautiful undergarments and finely crafted shoes. Most importantly, each doll wears a distinctive leather tag with a serial number to insure its collectibility as a limited edition series. La Cheri—an enchanting trio of showcase dolls that collectors will cherish for years! Tan colored designer package has the La Cheri logo in stunning silver lettering.

#4728 Asst. Pak 3

#4726 LA CHERI doll in burgundy

#4727 LA CHERI doll in navy blue

#4725 LA CHERI doll in pink

© Sekiguchi Co., Ltd. 1983

Asst. #4728 LA CHERI French Country Garden Collection

The 18" "La Cheri" collection of 1983 made by Sekiguchi of Japan for Mattel's "Collectors" grouping was limited to 1800 each. The doll standing is in all burgandy with blonde hair. Sitting left: Navy blue floral print with white dotted pinafore, straw hat with navy ribbon and has large pink flower on pinafore. right: in yellow floral, pink pinafore, reddish brown hair and a pink straw hat. Made in Japan for Mattel by Sekiguchi.

MATTEL
COLLECTOR
DOLLS

#4736 MARIKO MUSIC

#4737 MARIKO ART

#4732 MARIKO MIME

マリコ

MARIKO.

**Numbered limited edition series**

Mariko™— four of the most captivating dolls
in the collector doll world in a numbered
limited edition series. The Mariko dolls'
magnificent ivory complexions result from
a unique new material reminiscent of fine
porcelain. Fourteen inches tall, their bodies
are poseable and have been carefully designed
to create a lifelike appearance. Their fine
synthetic hair is crimped, colored and cut
into unique fashionable styles. Exquisitely
designed clothing with incomparable
originality and detail complete the Mariko
look. Finally, the dolls are tagged at the
wrist with a distinctive tag. The package
is triangular-shaped with a striking hand-
brushed logo. Mariko… their beauty and
complete originality will captivate collectors
for years to come. Mariko is magic!

#4471 Asst. Pak 4
#4732 Std. Pak 2
#4734 Std. Pak 2
#4736 Std. Pak 2
#4737 Std. Pak 2

#4734 MARIKO DRAMA

MATTEL

Asst. #4471 MARIKO Dolls

© Mattel, Inc. 1983. Hawthorne, CA 90250.
**PRINTED IN U.S.A.** All Rights Reserved.

© Sekiguchi Co., Ltd. 1983

14″ "Mariko" grouping made in Japan for Mattel's series of "Collector" dolls and limited to
1800 of each doll. Top: "Music" in lavender, blue and pink. "Art" in floral pattern dress with
white trim. Each have flowers in hair. Lower left: "Mime" in yellow, navy and red/white bow
in hair. Boy is "Drama" with stripe pants, black jacket, white hat with red band and red flower
and suspenders. Produced in "New material reminiscent of fine porcelain" reads the brochure.
Dolls range from boys red hair to yellow blonde and tosca blonde. These dolls designed by
Miss Akemi Watabe who for 25 years has been a fashion illustrator, in graphic arts, visual
design advisor and a free lance illustrator for children's books and magazines. The dolls are
made by Sekiguchi of Japan for Mattel, and this set was new in 1983.

15½″ "Queen Ann" with vinyl head, blue sleep eyes and rooted hair. Has plastic body and limbs and wears original, removable clothes. Marks: MAR-DEE CREATIONS, INC., on back and on tag. 1978. (Courtesy Marilyn Hitchcock)

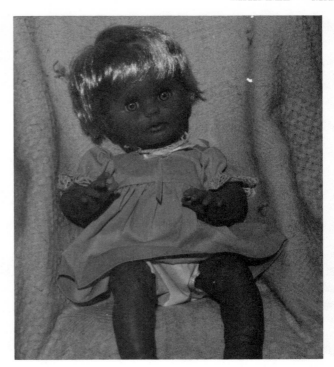

17″ "First Love." Marks: MARX 1978, on head but first appeared in 1979. Blue sleep eyes, rooted blonde hair, posable body with twist-and-turn waist and in original clothes. Excellent detail to hands and feet. Body is scented with Johnson's Baby Powder. (Courtesy Phyllis Teague)

17″ "First Love." Black version with brown sleep eyes and black rooted hair. 1978-1979. (Courtesy Shirley Merrill)

11″ "Sindy." Hard plastic body and hands. Vinyl arms, legs and head. Bendable arms and legs. High heel feet. Extra joints at waist and wrist. Posable head, painted blue eyes. Marks: "2 Gen 1077/033055X," on head. MADE IN HONG KONG, on lower back. Box: MARX TOYS. Sindy's horse: LOUIS MARX & CO/MCMLXVII/MADE IN U.S.A. F.A.O. Schwarz sells the Sindy doll (identical, but with sleep eyes) that is made in England.

5″ "Flowergirl." Orange, fat plastic body, arms, legs. Jointed waist, removable clothes, molded on shoes. Rooted hair, painted blue eyes. From Wizard of Oz. Marks: same as Mayor. (Courtesy Marie Ernst)

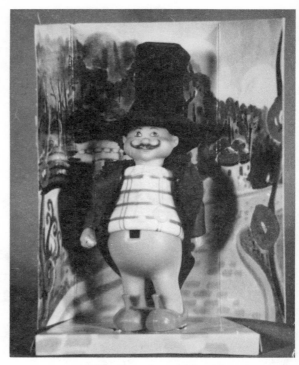

5″ "Mayor." Plastic with vinyl head. Removable coat and tall hat. Painted-on mustache. From Wizard of Oz. Marks: 1974/MGM INC. on head. MGM INC. 1976/MADE IN HONG KONG, on back. Made by Mego Co. (Courtesy Marie Ernst)

8″ "Grek of One Million B.C." Full plastic action figure. Vinyl head with rooted hair, painted eyes and molded beard with open/closed mouth and modeled teeth. Marks: MEGO CORP 1974/PAT. PEND./HONG KONG, on back. 1975 MEGO CORP. on head.

7½″ "Isis." Full action figure with painted blue eyes, rooted black hair and Isis symbol painted on forehead. Marks: 1976/FILMATION/A5500, on head. MEGO CORP./MCMLXXII/PAT. PENDING/MADE IN/HONG KONG, on back.

12½″ "Jaclyn Smith." Uses the "Cher" body with inset long lashes. Jointed waist and wrists. Marks: MEGO CORP. on head. MEGO CORP 1975/MADE IN HONG KONG, lower back.

12½″ "Suzanne Somers" as Chrissy of 'Three's Company." Vinyl head with inset lashes, open/closed mouth with painted teeth. Painted blue eyes. Plastic body and hands with bendable arms and legs of vinyl. Jointed waist. Early "Cher" body with extra long nails. Wears same dress in which "Cher" was issued in. Marks: THREE'S COMPANY, on head. MEGO CORP. 1975/MADE IN HONG KONG, lower back.

12½″ Lynda Carter as "Wonder Woman." Diana Prince outfit of Navy Uniform also included in package. Rigid plastic body and hands, rest in vinyl with jointed waist, wrists and ankles. Bending knees. Inset lashes and painted features. Painted on panties and top. Rooted hair. Marks: D.C. COMICS/INC. 1975, on head. MEGO CORP. 1975/MADE IN HONG KONG, on back.

7½″ "Richey and Potsy." Plastic and vinyl full action figures with molded hair and painted eyes. "Richey has striped shirt and "Potsy" has open/closed mouth. Marks: 1976 PARAMOUNT/PICTURES CORP, on heads. MEGO CORP 1974/REG. U.S. PAT. OFF/PAT.PENDING/HONG KONG, on backs. From T.V. Show "Happy Days."

225

6½″ "Teen Titan." This set includes: "Aqualad," "Kid Flash," "Wondergirl," and "Speedy." Jointed waist and knees. Rooted hair and painted eyes. Plasttic body and legs. Rigid vinyl arms. Vinyl head. Marks: NFP INC. 1976, on head. MEGO CORP. /REG. U.S.PAT. OFF/PAT. PENDING/HONG KONG, on back. Package: 1976 D.C. COMICS, INC.

9″ "Dale of Arden" of Flash Gordon group. Others include "Ming the Merciless" and "Dr. Zarkov." Plastic body and arms. Jointed elbows, wrists and waist. One-piece, posable vinyl legs with molded and painted on boots. Vinyl head with rooted hair, painted green eyes. Marks: KING FEATURES/SYN. INC. 1976. on head. 1977 MEGO CORP/MADE IN HONG KONG, on back.

9½″ "Ming the Merciless" of the Flash Gordon set. Plastic and vinyl full action figure. Original. Collar has been turned down so face can be seen. Bald head and excellent detailed ears. Comes with another helmet, sword, gun. Marks: KING FEATURES/SYN INC. 1976, on head. 1976 MEGO CORP./MADE IN HONG KONG, on back. Others in set: "Flash Gordon," "Dale Arden" and "Dr. Zarkov." Center is "Flash Gordon" and right is "Dr. Zarkov."

16″ "Baby Sez So." Plastic and vinyl with rooted hair, open/closed mouth with white painted between lips. Battery operated talker. Eyes are painted blue. Marks: MEGO CORP. 1976. May be original dress. (Courtesy Mr. Arthur Messer)

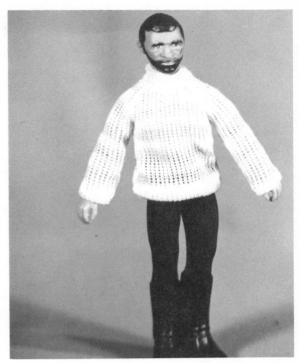

8″ "Chopper" from the "Starsky and Hutch" series. Full action figure. Has scar on cheek. All plastic with vinyl head. Marks: SPELLING/GOLDBERG PROD., on head. MEGO CORP/REG. US PAT. OFF/PAT. PENDING/HONG KONG, on back. 1975.

12½″ "Arcturian" from the "Star Trek" movies. Marks: PPC inside square, on head. MEGO CORP. 1977/MADE IN HONG KONG, on back. Put on market in 1979. Completely jointed action figure with extra joints at elbows, wrists, knees and ankles. Original. Arms and hands are painted brown. (Courtesy Renie Culp)

12½″ "Llia" from The "Star Trek" movie. Marks: PPC in a square on head. MEGO CORP. 1975/MADE IN HONG KONG, lower back. Marketed in 1979. Posable limbs and has bald head as character did in movie. (Courtesy Renie Culp)

12″ "Lenny & Squiggy" of the "LaVerne and Shirley Show" on T.V. Rigid vinyl body and limbs with no extra joints. Vinyl heads with molded hair and painted features. "Lenny" has open/closed mouth. Marks: PARAMOUNT PICTURES/CORPORATION, on heads. MEGO CORP./REG. U.S. PAT. OFF./PAT. PENDING/HONG KONG, on backs. 1977.

11½″ "Shirley." Plastic body with rigid vinyl legs. Vinyl head and arms. Rooted brown hair and painted blue eyes. Jointed waist. Marks: PARAMOUNT/PICT. CORP., on head. MEGO OF HONG KONG/1977, on back.

11½″ "Laverne." Plastic body with rigid vinyl legs. Vinyl head and arms. painted green eyes, open/closed mouth with painted teeth. Rooted hair, jointed waist. Marks: PARAMOUNT/PICT. CORP. on head. MEGO OF HONG KONG/1977/MADE IN HONG KONG. on back.

"KISS" - Gene has very long modelled tongue. Quality of the KISS clothing is above average. Marks same as other dolls in this group.

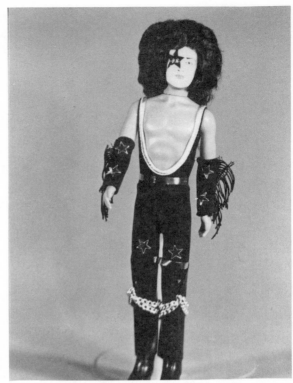

"KISS." Plastic bodies and hands, rest is vinyl. Jointed waists, bendable knees and painted eyes. Hair is rooted. Excellent quality to modelling. Marks: 1978 AUCOIN/M.G.M.T.INC. on heads. MEGO CORP. 1976/MADE IN HONG KONG, lower back. This one is Paul.

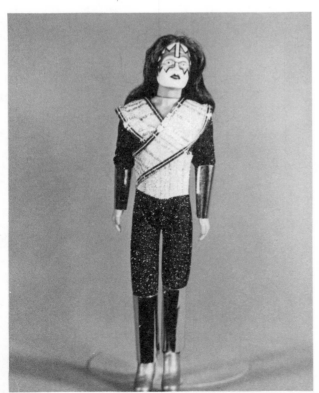

"KISS" - Ace. Holds head sharply back and head is modelled that way. Same marks as the other dolls in this group.

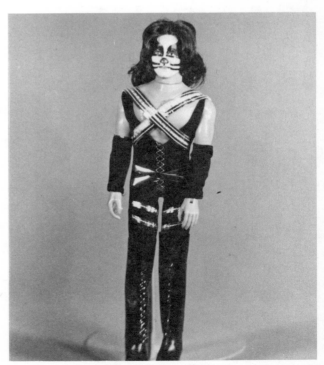

"KISS" - Peter. Has different body than other and it is modelled heavier and chunkier. Jointed at wrists, elbows, knees and ankles. Marks: 1978 AU-COIN/M.G.M.T. INC, on head. MEGO CORP. 1976/MADE IN HONG KONG, lower back.

12″ "Captain and Tennelle." She has same body as "Cher" with brown painted eyes and inset long lashes. Open/closed mouth with painted teeth. NO ears were modelled onto doll. Marks: MOONLIGHT &/MAGNOLIAS, INC. on head. He is full action figure that is all plastic with vinyl head. Marks: none on head. MEGO CORP. 1977/MADE IN HONG KONG, on back.

7¾″ "Chips-Ponch and Jon." Plastic action figures with painted black hands molded like a glove. Brown socks attached to lower legs of pants to allow boots to slide on/off easily. Molded hair and painted features. Comes with helmet and dark glasses. Marks: Ponch: MEGO CORP. 1974/REG. US PAT. OFF./PAT. PENDING/HONG KONG, both have this mark on bodies. Jon is marked: MGM/NC 1977, on head.

6″ "Puppet Love," "Prince Charming." Velour and cloth with vinyl head with rooted hair and painted green eyes. Very good quality. Marks: MEGO CORP./1977 on head. Stand is marked: PUPPET LOVE.

11½″ "Maddie Mod" by Mego. Plastic body and legs. Vinyl head and arms. Painted blue eyes. Rooted yellow hair that comes: long & straight, curled into a flip. Rather large nose. Jointed waist. Marks: 1974 MEGO, on head. MEGO CORP. MCMLIV/HONG KONG, on back.

0300    0408    0401    0402    0403

0410    0406    0407    0404    0409

#0400 Assortment          May be had individually or by assortment

13" "Angel" from Mel Cassons popular cartoon character and is all vinyl with inset glassene eyes. Shown in the various outfits that were available for her. Made by the M & S Doll Company. 1961.

1948 Internationals that are all cloth with mask faces which are oil painted. Made by Mollye Goldman of International Doll Company.

1948 Internationals by the Mollye International Doll Company. All cloth with mask faces which are oil painted. Mohair wigs in front only.

Mollye purchased dolls from many factories and companies and they were wigged and dressed at her factory. The tall doll at the far left is an Italian doll, all the small ones were made by the Junel Doll Company. The two, tall, all-composition dolls at the top right were made by the American Character Doll Company. The two top dolls which are tall, and the two small dolls next to them, are ballerinas.

20"-27" Internationals and Storybook dolls made in 1948. Each have composition heads with sleep eyes and all use the same head except the baby "French." It must be remembered that Mollye bought "blank" (unmarked) dolls and dressed them at her factory. The top three dolls are all composition and the lower three have cloth bodies and limbs.

Top Row: 21″ "Margaret Rose" and "Barbara Rose." Bottom row: 18″ "Peggy Rose," 24″ "Sherry Ann," and 14″ "Polly Rose." Brides of the "Rose Family." 1945 and 1946. Made by Mollye under the name Hollywood Cinema Fashions. All are composition. The "Peggy Rose" is "Sandra" made by Eugene Doll Company, and the others are from different companies.

The 1948 group of "Rose Family" Brides and Bridesmaids are: Top row: 23″ "Hedda Rose," 21″ "Margaret Rose" and 21″ unknown, non-Bride or Bridesmaid. The bottom row includes 11″ "Peggy Rose Bride" and "Polly Rose Bridesmaid" Also a 13″-14″ unknown (large straw hat) and left: three unknown 8″. The three 8″ to the right are Brides and Bridesmaids.

16", 18" and 21" sizes of "Kutey" with the girls on top row made of all composition and the babies are cloth and composition. Made by Mollye for the Hollywood Cinema Fashions in 1948. The maker of the dolls is unknown.

A group of 1948 babies that are 18" and 21". The lower far left doll is a Horsman, and the lower far right doll is by American Character. Made by Mollye under the name Hollywood Cinema Fashions. It must be remembered that Mollye purchased "blank" dolls from various companies to dress as she did not manufacturer dolls herself, but only designed and made the clothes. Dolls are all composition with cloth bodies.

These fat all cloth 27″ "Snow Babies" are dressed in red with black trim, peaked hats and sewn on white felt gloves. Yarn hair and face masks which are hand painted in oils. Mollye made is this set in mid-1940's under the name Hollywood Cinima Fashions. They came in 18″, 23″ and 27″ sizes.

The early Mollye Goldman "Raggedy Ann and Andy" were designed by her, had long arms with stitching at elbows. Hand written across the chest is their names and Mollye's signature. The heart is printed on.

It is not known if this advertising doll, either 10″ or 14″, was ever produced. The request came to Mollye Goldman by a jobber of Premuims, the Curtis Advertising Specialty Company in Dec. 1950 for one of their clients, which is also unknown. Photo by Newman-Schmidt. (File No. 50133C2).

25″ Shirley Temple-type made by Mollye during the mid-to late 1930's. The gown is pink with organdy trim. Replaced bonnet. Open mouth with teeth and blonde mohair wig. Both arms are bent at the elbows. Doll is all composition. Unmarked. (Courtesy Cookie Mullins)

Late 1940's doll in wardrobe case with extra clothes. Doll is all composition and most likely made by Horsman. Dark brown human hair wig with clothes designed and made by Mollye Goldman. Came in 14″, 17″ & 21″.

20″ All composition and unmarked. Brown sleep eyes, human hair wig with lashes and in original set. Original clothes are beautifully made. The gown is red and blue plaid with red cuffs and large brim bonnet. White lace trim on both. She wears pantaloons with three tiers of lace, and has lace on fine cotton slip attached to bodice. Red leatherette shoes with cutouts on sides. Made by Mollye in 1947. Name of dolls is unknown. Doll is most likely one made by the Arranbee Doll Co. (Courtesy June Schultz)

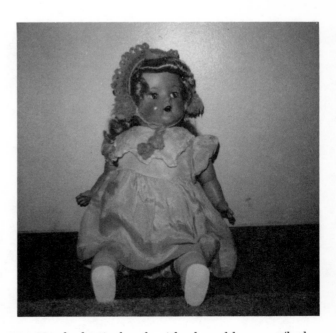

13″ Mollye Goldman tagged clothes on all composition toddler using an Ideal mold with a faint "Ideal" on head. Magnetic hands. Doll has brown sleep eyes and open mouth with teeth. (Courtesy June Schultz)

20″ Hard plastic head with sleep blue eyes/lashes. Open mouth with two upper teeth, felt tongue; long blonde wig. Cloth body with early vinyl arms and legs. Cryer in stomach. Made by Mollye. 1950. (Courtesy Dorothy Judge)

17″ "Little Miss" wave hair kit doll. All hard plastic with sleep blue eyes with eyeshadow, open mouth with upper teeth. Came in various dresses and hair color. Doll most likely made by Roberta Doll Co. or Valentine Doll Co. The doll will be unmarked.

20″ "Margaret Rose" Bridesmaid of 1950. All hard plastic walker and head turns from side to side as she walks. Glued-on wig, open mouth with upper teeth and a felt tongue. Blue sleep eyes. Unmarked. (Courtesy Carol Friend)

9″ One of the "Little Women" that is all vinyl, sleep blue eyes rooted hair and has freckles. Dressed in blue dots on white with red pinafore and ribbon in hair. Also came in reverse colors.

17″ (also came in 21″) "Cindy-Dancing Debutante" of 1950. All hard plastic with sleep eyes and eyeshadow, glued on wig. All original in satin and net gown, necklace and has flowers in hair. Bodice is lace trimmed as are the gloves.

8″ "Scotland." All vinyl with sleep eyes and rooted brown hair. 2nd and 3rd fingers are molded together and curled into palm. Came in 12 different International outfits and also as child with extra boxed clothes available for her.

12″ All vinyl used as International dolls. Sleep blue eyes, freckles and four lashes painted below the eyes. Came in 16 different outfits.

21″ Plastic body and legs with vinyl head and limbs. Doll is very much like the "Brickette" made by Vogue Doll Company, but does not have the jointed waist, green eyes, nor red hair. Closed smiling mouth, sleep blue eyes and rooted blonde hair.

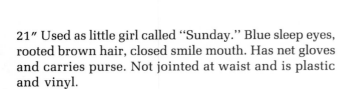

21″ Used as little girl called "Sunday." Blue sleep eyes, rooted brown hair, closed smile mouth. Has net gloves and carries purse. Not jointed at waist and is plastic and vinyl.

Nancy Ann Storybook doll of all bisque with jointed shoulders and one piece body, legs and head. 5″ "Colonial Dame" and #56 of American Girl Series. Floral print on white with blue bodice and side panniers with white trim. Blonde mohair wig and cap style bonnet. (Courtesy Pat Timmons)

5″ "Goldlilocks" and "Baby Bear" #128. Bisque with jointed shoulders and hips. Blonde hair. Wine color dress with white bodice and attached apron, wine color trim and polka dots. (Courtesy Pat Timmons)

5″ "Swedish" from Around the World Series. #37. Bisque with jointed shoulders and hips. Black gown with gold trim, multi-color attached apron and black peaked hat. Blonde hair. (Courtesy Pat Timmons)

5½″ "Daisy Belle" #179. Bisque with jointed shoulders only. Yellow satin and net gown with blonde hair and a daisy in net. (Courtesy Pat Timmons)

5½″ "Wednesday Child Full of Woe." #182. Bisque with jointed shoulders only. Gown is all red with pink flowers and ribbons in hair and carries rose pink hankie with white lace. Brown mohair wig. (Courtesy Pat Timmons)

3½″ #277 "Hush a By Baby," with layette on pillow and in original box. Pink organdy dress with white slip and diaper. Long pink dress and slip. Pillow is pink with white dots. Box is 8″ x 9″ with 2″ ruffle. (Courtesy Pat Timmons)

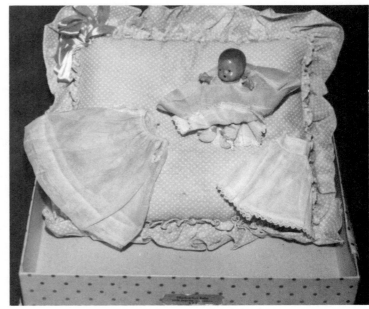

4½″ "Hush a By Baby Twins," Bisque with spray painted hair; jointed at shoulders and hips. Has layette which includes dresses, slips, and sweaters. In original oval box that is pink with white dots. (Courtesy Pat Timmons)

5½″ "Saturday's Child," "Must Work For a Living" #185. Bisque with jointed shoulders only. Red and white check gown with attached black apron with red trim. Black trim on gown. Red ribbon in dark brown hair. Carries a broom tied with red ribbon. (Courtesy Pat Timmons)

5″ "Western Miss" of the American Girl Series #58. Bisque and jointed at shoulders only. Black and white check gown with gold ribbon trim, attached white apron, black hat tied with gold ribbon. Blonde hair. (Courtesy Pat Timmons)

5½″ "First Day at School" #72 of "Commencement Series." Hard plastic with jointed shoulders, hips and neck. Blue sleep eyes, red mohair wig; dressed in pink and white check with pink apron, tied with white sash and with white lace trim. Pink ribbon in hair. (Courtesy Pat Timmons)

Bridal Series #86. Hard plastic with jointed shoulders, hips and neck. Range from 4½" to 7". "Bride" and "Groom," four "Bridemaids" with yellow, white, blue and pink gowns with imprinted gold stars. "Ringbearer" and "Flowergirl." "Groom" has painted hair and all have sleep eyes. (Courtesy Pat Timmons)

4½" Bridal Series #85 "Flowergirl." Hard plastic and jointed shoulders and hips. Sleep eyes. Dressed in pink with over lace bodice and attached apron. Painted long socks and shoes. Also #84 "Ring Bearer" with jointed shoulders and hips, sleep eyes blonde hair and dressed in pink. Short painted socks and shoes. In original boxes. (Courtesy Pat Timmons)

6" "Graduation" #74 of the Commencement Series. Hard plastic, jointed at shoulders, neck and hips. White gown with dots and lace trim. White ribbon used as trim also. (Courtesy Pat Timmons)

17″ "Nancy Ann." All hard plastic doll of 1955 or 1956. Sleep eyes with lashes. 2nd and 3rd fingers slightly curled and molded together. These dolls sometimes measure 18″, all are unmarked. Excellent quality clothes. This one appears to be a Bride as the gown is all white lace with satin hoop slip and with bouquet of flowers attached at waist instead of wrist. Pink ribbons in hair appear to be replaced. Veil missing. (Courtesy Donna Colopy)

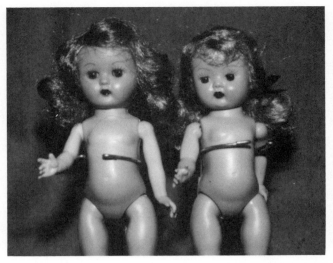

There is a slight difference in the face structure and the look-a-like doll has the 2nd and 3rd fingers molded together, where the "Muffie" has all separate fingers. (Courtesy Nancy Catlin)

Comparison of "Muffie" by Nancy Ann and a Muffie-look-a-like. The real "Muffie" is on the right. The body construction, legs and feet are identical; the arms are different. The eyes of the Muffie look-alike are cut wider and she is ¼″ taller (the head is actually longer. The "Muffie" is marked and the other is unmarked. Wigs are of the same material. Both dolls have painted and molded lashes and sleep eyes. (Courtesy Nancy Catlin)

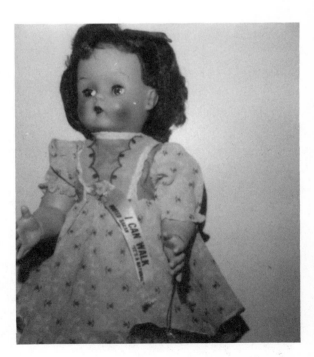

8″ "Muffie Groom" with flocked hair. All original with stripe pants, satin lapels, side snap vinyl shoes. All hard plastic, walker. (Courtesy June Sloniger)

19″ Walker. Vinyl head with rooted hair and sleep blue eyes. Hard plastic walker body and limbs. All original; has ribbon across front that says "I Can Walk". By the Natural Doll Co. 1956. (Courtesy Dorothy Judge)

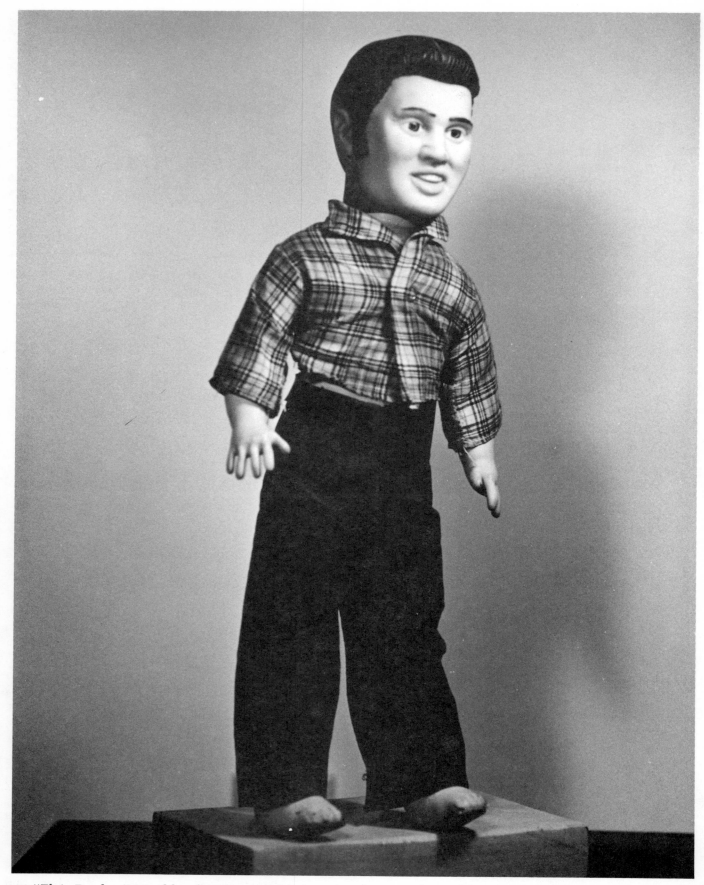

14″ "Elvis Presley." Vinyl head with molded hair, painted eyes and open/closed mouth. Latex body (Magic skin) that is all one piece. Marks: 1957 EPE, or will be marked ELVIS PRESLEY ENTERPRISES, on head. Original clothes, except front lace shoes missing. (Courtesy Rosalind Cranor)

12″ "MacAwful The Scot." All wood, painted, jointed, cloth clothes. Paper tag on back. MACAWFUL THE SCOT with TALENTOY inside drawn leaf. Other side: PUPPET & DRESSED FIGURE COPYRIGHT 1948/EFFANBEE DOLL CO.,/INTERNATIONAL COPYRIGHT RESERVED. Wood controls. The others in set: "Pim-Bo the Clown," "Toonga from the Congo," "Kilroy the Cop" and "Jambo the Jiver." In original box.

"Howdy Doody" was a star on N.B.C. television and is shown with his manipulator, Rhoda Mann. From "Quick" magazine, July 3, 1950.

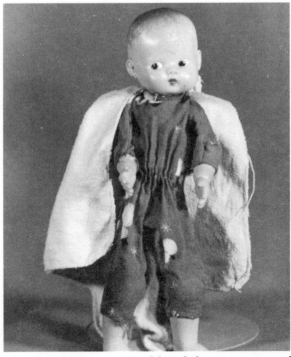

8″ "Superman" with stamped sponge rubber body. Clothes for Superman on one side and Clark Kent on the other. Vinyl head with molded hair, painted features. Marks: DC COMICS, INC./1979/SYNERGISTICS RESEARCH CORP./MADE IN HONG KONG, on back. (Author)

12″ Hand puppet. Vinyl head, lower arms and legs. Flannel body and blanket. Molded hair and painted eyes. Marks: IDEAL DOLL, on head.

10″ tall vinyl headed puppet made for the hand. Very well modelled and painted. Painted eyes. Puppet not marked. (Courtesy Phyllis Houston)

18″ Oriental puppet with cloth upper legs and wooden lower legs with black painted slippers. Very short wooden arms with both hands curled into fists. Heavy composition material head with excellent quality painted features, and high quality elaborate costume with beads and celluloid style sequins and fringe. Wig is apparently black horse hair. Unmarked.

11½″ "Wonderwoman" puppet. Vinyl head with excellent modeling. Jointed elbows, knees and ankles. Marks: MADISON LTD./MADE IN HONG KONG/PAT PEND. Painted on clothes except panties. Plastic controls.

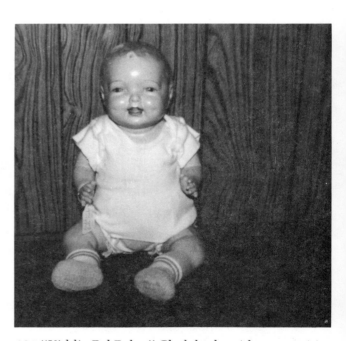

19″ "Kiddie Pal Baby." Cloth body with composition shoulder head, and limbs. The legs are disc jointed and arms strung through shoulderplate. Molded, painted hair, open/closed mouth with two upper teeth, smile and dimples. Marks: KIDDIE PAL BABY/REGAL DOLL MFG. CO. INC. Ca. 1926-1928. (Courtesy Jeannie Mauldin)

5¾″ "Lurch" of the T.V. show The Adams Family. Jointed at neck only and head marked: 1964 FILMWAYS T.V. PROD. INC. Painted, molded clothes and features. Rooted hair. Made by Remco. (Courtesy Shirley Pascuzzi)

12″ "Flying Superman." Has X-ray vision with battery operated eyes. Figure is unjointed. Came with Kryptonite rock and rope for "flying." 1979. Made by Remco. (Courtesy Shirley Pascuzzi)

8½″ "Rainbow." Vinyl head with rooted hair, painted features, rigid plastic body and limbs and has swivel waist. Medium high heel feet, ball jointed arms ad legs that are very posable. Excellent quality. Came with electronic computer center that has changeable computer cards that display make up, hair color and clothes changes. Also has extra clothes packaged with doll. Marks: REMCO 1979/HONG KONG, on head and back. Sold new for $29.95.

"The Proud Family." He has molded hair and she has rooted hair. Both have painted features with smiling mouths. The Mother can be made to look pregnant and has a maternity dress included. Marks: REMCO 1978. (Courtesy Phyllis Teague)

24″ "Daisy." Cloth body with composition head and limbs. Molded black hair, brown tin sleep eyes. Unmarked. Made by Rex Doll Co., N.Y. All original. (Courtesy Kay Bransky)

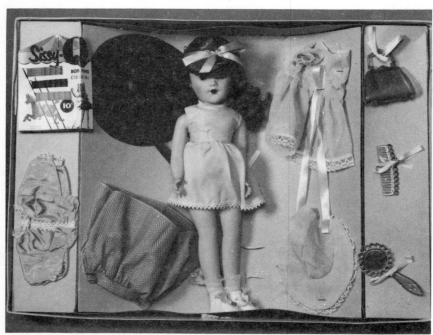

10″ "Sissy-Q." Bobby pin doll in original box with extra wardrobe. All hard plastic with sleep eyes and glued on long red wig. This is the "Roberta Lee" doll of 1954 in the smaller size. Doll is unmarked. Made by the Roberta Doll Co. (Courtesy Marjorie Uhl)

15½″ Hard plastic walker with wide spread legs. Open mouth with teeth, long blonde hair pulled up into a bun, and sleep blue eyes. Marks: MADE IN U.S.A. Ca. 1954. Made by Roberta Doll Co. (Courtesy Karen Miller)

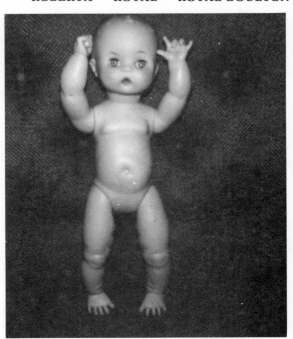

17″ All vinyl with molded hair, sleep eyes and open mouth. All fingers closed on right hand and 2nd and 3rd fingers curled on left hand. Has all toes very wide spread. Marks: ROYAL DOLL 1960, on head. ROYAL, on back (Courtesy Jeannie Mauldin)

18″ "Roxanne" doll from the T.V. show. She is all original and has her name on the camera. All hard plastic with glued on saran wig, sleep eyes and an open mouth with teeth. Original clothes. Doll is only marked with: "180," on the back. Made by the Roberta Doll Co. (Courtesy Virginia Jones)

In 1981 Royal Doulton put out these limited to 5000 world wide dolls dressed in Kate Greenaway clothes that were hand sewn by the Peggy Nesbit Company. Each is marked with the Royal Doulton backstamp. The head and hands are bisque and the dolls were designed by Eric Griffiths, the company's Art Director of sculpture. They are 12″ (suggested retail $175.00) and 8″ (suggested retail $125.00). Left to right: "Winter" in red and black, "Small Sister" in white with blue sash, "Bib Sister" in white with blue velvet sash and on hat, "Vera" in ecru with basket of flowers and "Little Model" in ecru cotton gown, blue velvet waist band, blue bonnet and burgandy short shawl. 1981.

This 1981 set of Victorian Birthday Dolls had a suggested retail for $125.00. Left to right: "Sunday's Child" in blue velvet and white muff, "Monday" blue cotton gown and hat with white apron, "Thursday" in navy sailor suit, "Tuesday" pink night dress and nightcap, long braids and holds Teddy Bear, "Wednesday" in printed gown and white pinafore, "Friday" in white with apron full of flowers, "Saturday" in maid's black gown, white apron and bonnet and holds duster. Dolls are 12".

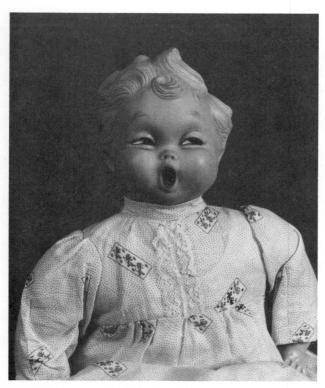

17" "Sleepy Head." Cloth body with vinyl head and excellent molded yellow hair, black painted eyes and wide yawning mouth. Vinyl arms and legs. Marks: RUSHTON, on head. 1958.

23" "Little Boy Blue." Stuffed sateen, felt shoes, vest and hat. Vinyl mask face, vinyl hands and 2nd and 3rd fingers curled into palm on left and all fingers spread apart on right. Painted features, molded hair in front and plush in back. LITTLE BOY BLUE tag and tag on side: RUSHTON STAR CREATION, ATLANTA, GA.

20″ "Sally Lou." All composition; original clothes. Jumper dress is pink and white check with white organdy bodice and sleeves and matching bonnet. Glassene sleep eyes/lashes. Made by Sally Lou Dolls, Newark, N.J. Right: 20″ "Baby Linda" All composition, but also came on cloth body with compo head and limbs. Also came with hard plastic head and latex body and limbs. 1945-1946. Made for Imperial Crown. (Page 146 of *Modern Collectors Dolls, Vol. 4)* (Courtesy Kay Bransky)

The 1964 Life Magazine carried an article and photos of the original Sasha doll made by designer and maker, Sasha Morgenthaler, which included this set of Eskimo children. The original designed dolls sold from $50.00 to $150.00 each. Mrs. Morgenthaler only made about 150 dolls per year. The molded were leased and sold to a firm in England that have been making the dolls continously since Mrs. Morgenthaler's death. (Photo by Fred Mayer)

16″ Sasha of 1981 and a Limited Edition dress of navy blue velvet. Blue painted eyes and incised "#763," on head. Only 5,000 made and came with certificate. (Courtesy Shirley Merrill)

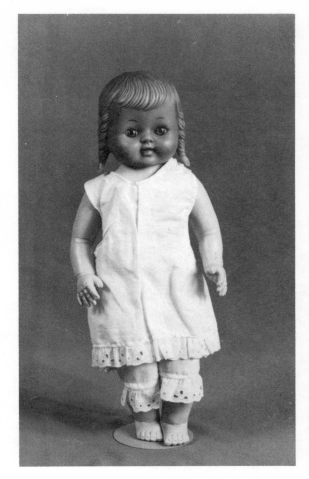

14″ "Playmate." Early vinyl head with molded hair that has bangs and has braids that hang down sides of face. Inset blue eyes. All stuffed vinyl body that is made in one piece. Unmarked. Made in 1955 by Sayco.

This is a listing of Miss America, and Miss Teen Age America. These dolls pop up from time to time, especially dolls of the 1950's and into the 1970's.

Miss America
1951: Yolanda Betbeze-Miss Alabama
1952: Colleen Hutchins-Miss Utah
1953: Neva Jane Langley-Miss Georgia
1954: Evelyn Ay-Miss Pennsylvania
1955: Lee Meriwether-Miss California
1956: Sharon Ritchie-Miss Colorado
1957: Marian McKnight-Miss South Carolina
1958: Marilyn Van Derbur-Miss Colorado
1959: Mary Ann Mobley-Miss Mississippi
1960: Lynda Lee Mead-Miss Mississippi
1961: Nancy Fleming-Miss Michigan
1962: Maria Fletcher-Miss North Carolina
1963: Jacquelyn Mayer-Miss Ohio
1964: Donna Axum-Miss Arkansas
1965: Vonda Kay Van Dyke-Miss Arizona
1966: Deborah Bryant-Miss Kansas
1967: Jane Jayroe-Miss Oklahoma
1968: Debra Dene Barnes-Miss Kansas
1969: Judith Ford-Miss Illinois
1970: Pamela Eldred-Miss Michigan
1971: Phyllis George-Miss Texas

Miss Teen Age America
1963: Darla Banks
1964: Jeanine Zavrel
1965: Carolyn Mignini
1966: Collette Daiute
1967: Sandy Roberts
1968: Stephanie Crane
1969: Melissa Babish
1970: Debbie Patton
1971: Rewa Walsh
1972: Colleen Fitzpatrick
1973: Melissa Gabrath
1974: Lori Matsukawa
1975: Karen Peterson
1976: Cathy Durden

8″ "Miss America" by the Sayco Doll Corp. and endorsed by the Miss America Pagent. (No. 2000). No marks on body and a small "s," on neck. Vinyl head with platinum rooted hair and blue sleep eyes/molded lashes. Hard plastic body and limbs. Jointed knees & a walker, with head moving as she walks. Shown in original ballerina outfit that is white with red trim, red flowers at waist and red satin ballet slippers. 1959. (Courtesy Donnie Durant)

10½″ "Miss America." Vinyl with rooted hair, blue sleep eyes wi molded lashes, pearl earrings, pearlized crown, original dress wi purple banner: MISS AMERICA attached. High heel feet, nylons an has painted toe and finger nails. Head is marked: SAYCO DOLL. 19 (Courtesy Shirley Pascuzzi)

Denim jeans with orange sweater and brown and white saddle shoes are originals for the "Miss America" Doll by Sayco. (Courtesy Donnie Durant)

Tennis outfit for the Sayco "Miss America". Turquoise and white stripe shorts and white blouse. (Courtesy Donnie Durant)

Blue velvet skating outfit with red taffeta lined skirt and rabbit fur trim. Silver skates. Original to Sayco's "Miss America" doll. (Courtesy Donnie Durant)

14″ "Asian." Brown skin tones with painted features, black rooted hair. Marks: SHINDANA TOYS 1976, on head. Not original clothes. (Courtesy Shirley Merrill)

11½″ "Adventure Girl" by Shillman and just marked HONG KONG on head. Plastic and vinyl. Long inset lashes. Frosted rooted hair, blue painted eyes & open/closed mouth. Full action figure with lower torso painted white. High heel feet. (Courtesy Marie Ernst)

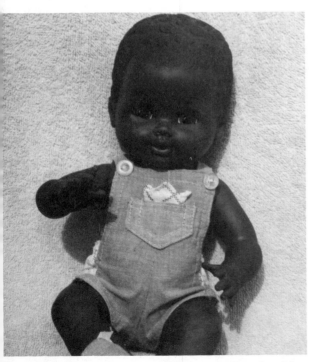

1½″ "Zuri." All heavy vinyl and jointed at shoulders, neck and hips. Marks: SHINDANA TOYS 1972/DIV. PER. BOOTS STRAP INC. Original clothes. Courtesy Mrs. Frank Miller)

12½″ Little Friends (Hispanic) by Shindana. All vinyl that is pale brown with large painted brown eyes. Open mouth/nurser. Rooted hair. Marks: SHINDANA TOYS 1976, on head. Three in series: Asian, Black and Hispanic. (Courtesy Carol Friend)

12″ Promotional doll made of vinyl and jointed. Dressed in basic dress trimmed with lace, bottle also included. Open mouth/nurser. Marks: SHINDANA 1977, on head.

12″ "Baby Tasha." All vinyl with rooted hair, sleep brown eyes, open mouth/nurser and comes with bottle, comb and brush. Dressed in original red print two piece blouse and skirt with contrasting trim. 1978 Shindana Toys Inc.

9½″ "Julius (Dr. J.) Erving." Full action figure with molded hair and painted features. Dressed in basketball uniform including shorts, tank top, socks, shoes and pads. Basketball also included. 1977 Shindana Toys, Inc.

9½″ "O.J. Simpson," All American Quarterback. Full action figure and basic doll came with pro outfit, complete with helmet, shoulder pads, jersey pants, two tone football shoes, striped socks and football. 1975 O.J. Simpson Enterprises, Inc. 1975 Shindana Toys. Molded hair and painted features.

11½″ "Disco Wanda." Plastic body with jointed waist. Vinyl arms, leg and head. Bendable knees. Painted brown eyes. Wide open/closed mouth with painted teeth. Uses old Barbie mold. Marks: HONG KONG, on back. Comes in various outfits and there is also a brown Disco Juanita. Made by Shindana.

7¾″ "Little Treasures." All plastic with glued on wigs, vivid blue sleep eyes. Extremely similar to the Madame Alexander molds. Marks: MADE IN HONG KONG, on back. Box: LITTLE TREASURES/SINGER CRAFTS PETERSON N.J. 07501. Costumes designed and manufactured in U.S.A. Plastic parts made in Hong Kong. Printed and packaged in U.S.A.

16″ "Terri Lee." All original with white hair and white ball gown of satin and net with lace insert sleeves and trim at hemline. (Courtesy May Williams)

16″ "Terri Lee" in black and white check bathing suit and has her own swimming ring that is blue and yellow with her name imprinted on it. (Courtesy June Schultz)

9″ Black "Linda Baby." All early vinyl with painted black brush stroked hair over molded hair, brown painted eyes. Curled toes and individual fingers. Three lower painted lashes and two upper, at corners of eyes. Has tagged pink satin coat and bonnet that are tagged. 1950's. (Courtesy Betty Casteel)

18″ Black Troll that is all vinyl with jointed neck only, inset glassene eyes/lashes and marked: DAM THINGS EST. 1964, on head. (Courtesy Virginia Jones)

14″ Cloth body Troll with vinyl head and hands. Inset glassene eyes. Body tag: IDEAL, in oval. SCANDINAVIAN ENTERPRISES, on head. (Courtesy Virginia Jones)

4½″ "Santa" Troll that is unjointed, rooted beard, vinyl inset eyes with painted pupil. Unjointed and unmarked. (Courtesy Virginia Jones)

11″ Cloth body troll with sewn on underclothes and removable top. Inset blue eyes and vinyl head. Marks: SCANDINAVIA, on head. (Courtesy Kathy Feagans)

12″ Very large and fat (10″ across) Santa Troll dressed in red and white with white hair. All vinyl with jointed neck and inset green eyes. Marks: DAM THINGS ESTABLISHMENT 1964 on foot. (Courtesy Kathy Feagans)

7″ "Brother Bear Leprechaun" and "Willy Fox." All vinyl with jointed necks. Made by Leprechaun, Ltd. Dublin, Ireland. 1970. Inset glassene eyes and comes with International Passport. Original. The fox has fur down the stomach area. (Courtesy June Schultz)

8″ "Monkey" All vinyl and jointed at neck only, large round inset eyes, original clothes and marked: U.S.A., on one foot. R. SHEKTER 1966, on other. (Courtesy Virginia Jones)

3″ "Cow" that is all vinyl and unjointed with large inset glassene eyes. Unmarked. (Courtesy Virginia Jones)

3″ "Donkey" that is all vinyl and unjointed with original felt "clothes." Inset glassene eyes. (Courtesy Virginia Jones)

3" "Elephant." All vinyl with no joints, inset glassene eyes. (Courtesy Virginia Jones)

7" "Viking." Inset glassene eyes, molded tooth and helmet. Glued on rabbit fur beard, original clothes. Marks: JOHN VISSIN/DENMARK. (Courtesy Virginia Jones)

2½" Troll with yellow hair, all vinyl and sitting down in molded position, very pointed ears. Original outift is blue felt with silver collar. Has two dark long lashes at sides of eyes. Marks: ROY DES OF FLORIDA. Ca. 1960's (Courtesy Kathy Feagans)

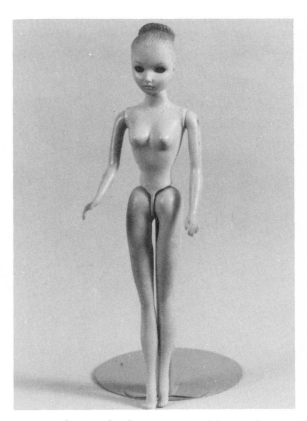

11½" "Judy" with sleep eyes/molded lashes and molded hair with bun. Rigid body with vinyl head and limbs. Has non-benable knees, a posable head and is excellent quality. The painted- eye version with rooted hair is called "Suzette," and there is also a sleep eyed version with rooted hair.

3″ Baby in 2½″ tall foot. One piece vinyl body and limbs. Jointed at neck only. Painted blue eyes to the side. No marks on doll or foot. Box: TOE-KINS-UNEEDA.

7½″ "Brenda Breyer." All vinyl with posable arms and legs. Breyer horses are exceptional and sold through fine toy stores and this is first doll ever made for them. Doll was made by Unger Toys and is unmarked.

5″ on left that is all purple and only jointed at neck and shoulders. Blue "crystal" dome to head. Marks: 1979/UNIV. STUDIOS/HONG KONG, on back. Part of the movie "The Black Hole." Right is 4″ Ernest Borgnine from the same movie with the same marks. Fully jointed action figure and has molded black hair.

Left: 4½″ All lavender monster jointed at shoulders and hips, attached purple back of head and removable lavender "gown." Marks: 1979/UNIV. STUDIOS/HONG KONG on back. From the movie "The Black Hole." Right: 3¾″ green monster with four arms and jointed at hips and shoulders. Detachable yellow net jacket. Marks are the same only located on side of right leg.

8″ "Red Riding Hood Toodles." All composition with painted blue eyes to side and glued-on blonde wig. Red/white print dress, red cape and black shoes with white socks. Carries basket of yellow flowers. Marks: VOGUE, on back. Ca. 1940's. (Courtesy Roberta Lago)

8″ "Tootles." All composition with straight arms, blue painted side glancing eyes, strawberry blonde wigs over molded hair and marked: VOGUE, on backs. The matching outfits are burnt orange knit overalls/yellow felt squirrel, multi-color cotton body suits and caps trimmed with red and yellow felt flowers. The shoes are replaced. Folded tag sewn on outside of overalls, white letters on blue background. (Courtesy Margaret Mandel)

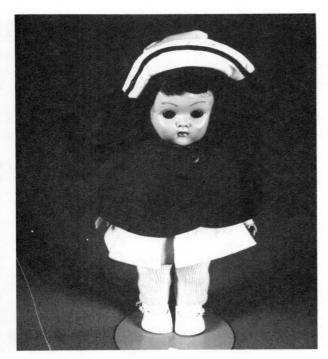

8″ "Ginny." All hard plastic with straight legs, non-walker and has no eyelids. White nurse uniform and cap with blue cape and trim. Replaced knit hose.

8″ "Ginny." All hard plastic, painted lashes, blonde wig; all original. Pink dotted dress trimmed in white eyelette, pink bow stapled to head. Marks: VOGUE, back of head and VOGUE DOLL, on back (Courtesy Shirley Merrill)

8" "Ginny." All hard plastic, straight leg, non-walker, no eyelids/painted lashes. Original clothes include zippered body suit, felt skirt and hat. Red glued on wig, brown sleep eyes. (Courtesy Michelle Freeman) (Photo by Sally Freeman)

7¼" Ginny-type shown with a real Ginny made by Vogue. The non-Ginny is marked: ENGLAND. (Courtesy Sally Freeman)

8" Ginny "Country Fair." Walker, painted eyelashes, gown that is floral print, white blouse and black bodice and trim. Straw hat with flowers. 1958. This doll also came with braided hair.

8" "Ginny." Hard plastic with vinyl head, blue sleep eyes, dark brown rooted hair and marked: GINNY on head; GINNY VOGUE DOLLS INC. PAT. NO. 2687534, on back. Made in U.S.A. All original. Has jointed knees. (Courtesy Shirley Merrill)

8″ "Ginny." Hard plastic with jointed knees and vinyl head with blonde rooted hair, sleep eyes and all original. Marks: GINNY, on head. GINNY, VOGUE DOLL INC. PAT. NO. 2687534. MADE IN U.S.A., on back. (Courtesy Shirley Merrill)

16″ "Hug A Bye Baby" 1975. Marks: VOGUE/1975, on head. Cloth body with vinyl head, arms and legs. Rooted white hair and very large round sleep eyes. Three fingers on one hand molded curled and all fingers on other molded curled with 1st finger and thumb touching. Original white eyelette dress and panties.

14″ "Baby Burps." All vinyl and has full joints, rooted black hair on Black doll and blonde hair on other. Painted eyes, dolls are open mouth/nursers and can blow bubbles and burp. Marks: 1975 LESNEY MADE IN HONG KONG. Back of box: BABY BURPS. VOGUE DOLLS MADE WITH LOVE. (Courtesy Jeannie Mauldin)

16″ "Baby Wide Eyes." All vinyl with very large brown sleep eyes/lashes. Dark rooted hair. All original. Marks: VOGUE 1976, on head. (Courtesy Shirley Merrill)

15″ "Bath Tub Baby." All vinyl with deeply detailed molded yellow hair, large round painted eyes. Came dressed in terry cloth panties and jacket with hood; have wash clothes. Marked: VOGUE DOLL 1974, on head. There is also a 10″ Black baby that is marked: VOGUE DOLL, on head and back. (Courtesy Sally Freeman)

8″ "Ginny." Blonde rooted hair and blue sleep eyes. All vinyl and fully jointed. Original clothes. Marks: 1979 VOGUE DOLLS INC./MOONACHIE N.J./MADE IN HONG KONG. (Courtesy Wendi Miller)

8″ "Ginnette." Vinyl with sleep eyes. Marks: 4/GINNY/VOGUE DOLLS/ 1977, on head. 1978 VOGUE DOLLS INC/MOONACHIE N.J./MADE IN HONG KONG, on back.

The new Ginny prices seem to depend on the color of the boxes. In this area the following colors/prices were evident: Green-$4.97, pink-$5.97 and blue-$3.97.

8″ "Ginny." Vinyl, brunette hair, blue sleep eyes. Fully jointed. Marks: 1979 VOGUE DOLLS INC./MOON-ACHIE N.J./MADE IN HONG KONG. (Courtesy Karen Miller)

8″ "Ginny." Brunette rooted hair, sleep blue eyes. All vinyl and fully jointed. Original clothes. Marks: 1979 VOGUE DOLLS INC/MOONACHIE N.J./MADE IN HONG KONG. (Courtesy Karen Miller)

18″ Re-issued "Brickette" with very curly "modern" hairdo rooted, sleep eyes and all original clothes. The re-issue included many hair and eye colors. 1979-1980.

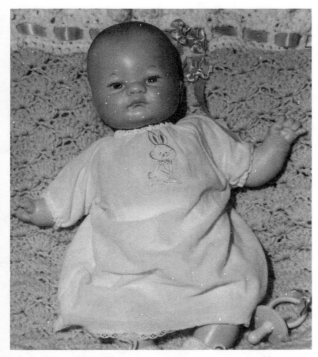

"Welcome Home Baby" with cloth body and vinyl head and limbs. Blue painted eyes, lightly painted hair and closed mouth. All fingers of both hands curled and 1st fingers touching thumbs. (Courtesy Phyllis Teague)

20″ "Welcome Home Baby Turns Two" by Vogue Dolls. Has one piece body of foam, sleep blue eyes and soft, fluffy, rooted hair. Original in pink and white. Vinyl heads and limbs that have excellent modeling. (Courtesy Phyllis Teague)

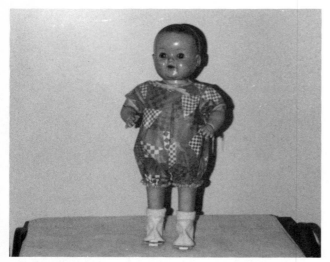

21″ "Walkalon" key wind walker. All hard plastic with molded brown hair, sleep eyes. Turns head and moves it's arms as it walks. Feet have roller and molded leather shoes. Marked: FOR SERVICE: SEND TO WALKALON MFG. CHICAGO 18 on back. (Courtesy Ann Wencel)

8″ "China Ginny Bride." Plastic body and legs with vinyl arms and head. Dark skin tones with oval shape painted eyes. Rooted black hair with full bangs. Ornate costume, metal head gear with red tassels. Marks: GINNY/VOGUE DOLL/1977. The Brides were released for just a short time in 1982 and included: Mexico, France, Germany, American, Egypt, Israel, Poland, England, Brazil, Turkey, Ireland and China.

"Wee Three" made for Woolworth/Woolco. Box is marked: ALL COPYRIGHTS RESERVED "HUNTER." All the dolls are marked HONG KONG. She has jointed knees and waist; painted blue eyes. He has painted brown eyes. All have rooted hair. The man also has jointed waist and knees. The baby is all one piece rigid vinyl, except the head which is softer vinyl (jointed at neck only) He is 9½″, she-8½″ and baby is 3″.

Shows the "Wee Three Yacht Club" family in their closed case.

20″ Vinyl character head with sleep blue eyes/lashes and painted lashes below the eyes. Closed mouth with slight smile. Rooted very orange hair with left side part and right side pulled back. Excellent detail ears. Hard plastic body with jointed knees and walker legs. Arms raise to shoulder only. In original pink/white check dress that is cotton and has attached cotton slip. White organdy pinafore. Marks: W.L. WILSON, on head. He may have been the designer by the same name for Playland Toy Corp. and dolls name is "Caroline Kay" Pat. #114,706 taken out in February 23, 1952. (Author)

17″ "Caroline." Cloth body and bisque head and limbs. Painted eyes and glued on wig. Original clothes. Sculptured and made by Beatrice Wright. Only 12 of this doll have been made. 1982-1983. (Courtesy Beatrice Wright)

14″ "Valarie." Plastic body and legs with vinyl head and arms. Rooted hair and brown painted eyes to the side. Very excellent modeling to facial features. Dressed in two piece yellow satin outfit. Marks: BEATRICE WRIGHT, on head. 1980's. (Courtesy Beatrice Wright)

# Index

278

# Price Guide

All dolls are priced as to condition shown in photograph. Letters may be shown along with prices, and the following are explanations:

N.O. – not original  R.W. – replaced wig  I.A. – item added
I.M. – item missing  B. – bad condition  S.A. – still available

| Page | Description | Price | Page | Description | Price |
|---|---|---|---|---|---|
| 6 | Norwegian | 150.00 | 23 | Princess Elizabeth | 700.00 |
| 6 | Campbell Kid (N.O.) | 550.00 | 23 | Margaret O'Brien (I.A.) | 900.00 |
| 6 | Ma-Lou | 95.00 | 23 | Babs the Skater, Sonja Henie | (each) 550.00 |
| 6 | Buttons | 300.00 | 23 | Maggie | 575.00 |
| 7 | Country Girl | 125.00 | 24 | Godey Group Girl | 850.00 |
| 7 | Merry, Minx & Mike | (each) 25.00 | 24 | Godey Group Boy | 950.00 |
| 8 | Hanes Baby | 150.00 up | 24 | Polly Pigtails | 675.00 |
| 8 | 13" Poppin' Fresh | 6.00 | 24 | Treena Ballerina | 475.00 |
| 8 | 14" Poppin' Fresh | 7.00 | 25 | Miss Flora McFlimsey | 600.00 |
| 8 | Pogo and Friends | (each) 4.00 | 25 | Peter Pan | 650.00 |
| 9 | Doodles | 9.00 | 25 | Scarlett | 750.00 |
| 9 | Mr. Peanut | (each) 30.00 | 25 | Agatha | 1,000.00 up |
| 10 | Jolly Green Giant | 20.00 | 26 | Quiz-kin Bride and Groom | (each) 750.00 up |
| 10 | Elsie the Cow | 95.00 | 26 | Alexanderkins, pink dress | 375.00 up |
| 10 | Big Boy | 7.00 | 26 | Wendy | (each) 375.00 |
| 11 | 16" Dolly | 8.00 | 26 | Little Southern Girl | 1,300.00 |
| 11 | Dolly and Big Boy | (each) 8.00 | 27 | Victoria | 1,300.00 |
| 12 | Snap, Crackle and Pop | (set) 10.00 | 27 | Straight Leg Walker | 350.00 up |
| 12 | Ronald McDonald | 30.00 | 27 | Wendy | 300.00 up |
| 12 | Burger King | 45.00 | 28 | Queen | 1,400.00 |
| 12 | Diaparene Baby | 6.00 | 28 | Dude Ranch | 900.00 |
| 13 | Gerber Babies: | | 28 | Tea Party | 350.00 |
| | White | 45.00 | 29 | "Hot Morning," 8" bend knee | 300.00 |
| | Black | 55.00 | 29 | Bride and Bridesmaids | 350.00 up |
| 13 | 1936 | 115.00 | 29 | Little Godey | 1,200.00 up |
| 13 | Arrow | 55.00 | 29 | Romeo and Juliet | 1,500.00 up |
| 13 | Sun Rubber | 60.00 | 30 | Bo Peep | 650.00 |
| 13 | Atlanta, 1979–80: | | 31 | Hansel and Gretel | 700.00 up |
| | White | 50.00 | 31 | Alice in Wonderland | 600.00 up |
| | Black | 60.00 | 31 | Cissy Secretary | 425.00 |
| 13 | Bisque | 300.00 | 31 | 8" Alexanderkin, graduation gown | 350.00 up |
| 13 | Porcelain | 250.00 | 32 | Southern Belle | 1,400.00 |
| 14 | Drink-and-Wet Gerber Baby | 75.00 | 32 | Others, Alexander-kins | 275.00 up |
| 14 | 21" Mermaid | 150.00 | 33 | 8" Alexander-kin | 350.00 up |
| 15 | Teeny Twinkle | 550.00 | 33 | Wendy "Goes Calling" | 350.00 |
| 15 | Boy | 650.00 up | 33 | Cissy Bride w/crown | 475.00 |
| 15 | Lively Cherub Baby | 350.00 | 33 | Cissy Bride w/gloves | 450.00 |
| 16 | Dottie Dumbunnie | 500.00 | 34 | "Time For School" | 275.00 |
| 16 | Posey Pet | 400.00 up | 34 | "Dressed For A Hot Morning" | 250.00 up |
| 17 | American Tot | 325.00 up | 34 | Alexanderkin #321 | 250.00 up |
| 17 | 7½" Lenci | 165.00 | 34 | Bend Knee Walker #676 | 300.00 up |
| 17 | 13" oil cloth | 400.00 | 34 | Maggie Mix-up | 600.00 up |
| 17 | Pitty Pat | 525.00 | 34 | India | 100.00 |
| 18 | Betty | 250.00 | 35 | Cissette | 500.00 up |
| 18 | Dionne Quints, basket | 1,400.00 | 35 | Cissette Bridesmaid | 500.00 up |
| 18 | Dionne Quints, wooden bed | 1,400.00 | 35 | Cissette-Lady Hamilton | 650.00 |
| 18 | Dr. Dafoe | 800.00 | 35 | Cabana | 250.00 up |
| 19 | 8" Dionne Quint toddlers | 1,600.00 | 36 | Walker in Pegnoir set | 200.00 up |
| 19 | 7½" Dionne babies with furniture | 1,600.00 | 36 | "May Day" | 350.00 up |
| 20 | Princess | 750.00 | 36 | Walker #0431 | 275.00 up |
| 20 | 9" China | 225.00 | 36 | Cissette | 265.00 up |
| 20 | Madelaine Du Bain | 500.00 | 37 | Enchanted Doll | 325.00 |
| 21 | Three Little Pigs | (each) 450.00 | 38 | Enchanted Doll | 350.00 |
| 21 | Wendy Ann | 350.00 | 38 | Fairy Godmother | 350.00 |
| 21 | Snow White | 400.00 | 38 | Little Genius | 250.00 up |
| 22 | 21" Sonja Henie | 700.00 | 38 | Barbara Jane, Penny face | 425.00 |
| 22 | 18" Sonja Henie | 600.00 | 39 | Bonnie (I.M.) | 145.00 |
| 22 | 15" Sonja Henie | 475.00 | 39 | Mimi | 850.00 up |

| Page | Description | Price |
|---|---|---|
| 158 | Nurse | 250.00 up |
| 158 | Miss Revlon | 185.00 |
| 158 | 12" (N.O.) | 15.00 |
| 158 | Betsy Wetsy (N.O.) | 50.00 |
| 159 | Bye Bye Baby | 350.00 up |
| 159 | Penny Playpal | 175.00 |
| 159 | Susy Playpal (N.O.) | 165.00 |
| 160 | 24" Betsy Wetsy (n.O.) | 45.00 |
| 160 | Pebbles and Bam Bam | 20.00 |
| 160 | Daddy's Girl | 850.00 up |
| 161 | Jet Set | (no price available) |
| 162 | Baby Belly Button | (each) 15.00 |
| 164 | First Crissy | 145.00 |
| 164 | Black Crissy | 125.00 |
| 164 | Talking Crissy | 85.00 |
| 164 | Talky Velvet | 70.00 |
| 165 | Movin' Crissy | 75.00 |
| 165 | Black Crissy | 125.00 |
| 165 | Kerry | 75.00 |
| 165 | Cinnamon | 70.00 |
| 165 | Black Cinnamon | 125.00 |
| 165 | Look Around Crissy | 60.00 |
| 165 | Black Look Around Crissy | 145.00 |
| 165 | Look Around Velvet | 60.00 |
| 165 | Black Look Around Velvet | 70.00 |
| 166 | Crissy | 60.00 |
| 166 | Velvet | 60.00 |
| 166 | Black Velvet | 125.00 |
| 166 | Movin' Velvet | 65.00 |
| 166 | Black Movin' Velvet | 145.00 |
| 166 | Dina | 90.00 |
| 166 | Brandi | 80.00 |
| 167 | Blue Eye Cricket | 80.00 |
| 167 | Cricket | 60.00 |
| 167 | Posin' Tressy | 75.00 |
| 167 | Tressy | 75.00 |
| 167 | Black Tressy | 125.00 |
| 167 | Baby Crissy | 65.00 |
| 167 | Black Baby Crissy | 85.00 |
| 168 | Curler Crissy | 55.00 |
| 168 | Black Curler Crissy | 60.00 |
| 168 | Velvet Braider | 55.00 |
| 168 | Black Velvet Braider | 75.00 |
| 168 | Velvet Daisy | 50.00 |
| 168 | Black Velvet Daisy | 75.00 |
| 168 | Twirly Beads Crissy | 50.00 |
| 168 | Black Twirly Beads Crissy | 85.00 |
| 169 | Cinnamon | 70.00 |
| 169 | Black Cinnamon | 125.00 |
| 169 | Tara | 50.00 |
| 170 | Mia | 75.00 |
| 170 | Magic Hair Crissy | 60.00 |
| 170 | Black Magic Hair Crissy | 90.00 |
| 170 | Dorothy Hamill | 28.00 |
| 170 | Suntan Dodie | 30.00 |
| 170 | Andy Gibb | 25.00 |
| 170 | Black Tuesday Taylor | 40.00 |
| 171 | Tuesday Taylor | 30.00 |
| 171 | My Bottle Baby | 16.00 |
| 171 | New Baby Crissy | 40.00 |
| 171 | New Velvet | 30.00 |
| 172 | Laura and Robin | (no price available) |
| 172 | Loni Anderson | (no price available) |
| 173 | Angel Babies | (no price available) |
| 174 | Victorian Ladies | (no price available) |
| 175 | Southern Girl | 100.00 |
| 175 | 20" Shirley | 750.00 |
| 175 | 15" Shirley/trunk | 700.00 |
| 175 | 20" | 765.00 |
| 176 | 18" Shirley | 685.00 |

| Page | Description | Price |
|---|---|---|
| 176 | 25" Shirley | 900.00 |
| 176 | 27" Shirley | 1,100.00 up |
| 177 | 19" Shirley | 685.00 |
| 178 | 36" Shirley | 1,800.00 up |
| 179 | 11" Shirley Temple | (each) 30.00 |
| 180 | Shirley Temple | (each) 30.00 |
| 181 | 20" | 55.00 |
| 181 | 22" | 95.00 |
| 181 | 5½" Baby | 6.00 |
| 181 | 7" Baby | 9.00 |
| 182 | 2" Baby | 4.00 |
| 182 | 11" Junel | 95.00 |
| 182 | 13" Iodine | 145.00 |
| 182 | 18" Iodine | 185.00 |
| 182 | 21" Iodine | 225.00 |
| 183 | 14" Rags to Riches | 65.00 |
| 183 | 20" Rags to Riches | 85.00 |
| 184 | Lolita | 85.00 |
| 184 | Baby Won't Let Go | 25.00 |
| 184 | Oscar Goldman | 20.00 |
| 184 | Armstrong | 12.00 |
| 185 | Shaun Cassidy | 25.00 |
| 185 | Parker Stevenson | 25.00 |
| 185 | Boba-Fett | 125.00 up |
| 185 | Darth Vader | 90.00 |
| 186 | Princess Leia | 90.00 |
| 186 | Luke Skywalker | 85.00 |
| 186 | International Velvet | 50.00 |
| 187 | Darcie | 40.00 |
| 187 | Erica | 45.00 |
| 187 | Dana | 40.00 |
| 188 | Sour Grapes | 10.00 |
| 188 | Kuddles | 15.00 |
| 188 | Cinderella | 20.00 |
| 188 | Betsy Clark | 10.00 |
| 189 | Gnome | 6.00 |
| 189 | Laura and Carrie | (each) 25.00 |
| 189 | Seahawk | 10.00 |
| 189 | Annie | 15.00 |
| 190 | Daddy Warbucks | 25.00 |
| 190 | Miss Hannigan | 25.00 |
| 190 | Punjab | 30.00 |
| 190 | Molly | 25.00 |
| 191 | Buddy Lee | 300.00 up |
| 191 | 11" | 15.00 |
| 191 | 22" | 40.00 |
| 191 | Angel | 16.00 |
| 192 | Jeannie | (each) 85.00 |
| 192 | Phantom & Hunchback | (each) 10.00 |
| 192 | 20" (N.O.) | 185.00 |
| 192 | 22" (N.O.) | 125.00 |
| 193 | 23" (N.O.) | 100.00 |
| 193 | Dolly Sunshine | 285.00 |
| 193 | 16" | 75.00 |
| 193 | 12" | (pair) 90.00 |
| 194 | 12" (I.A.) | 30.00 |
| 194 | 17" (I.A.) | 125.00 |
| 194 | 8" Bridal Party | (each) 30.00 |
| 195 | Rabbit | 27.00 |
| 195 | Scrappy | 300.00 up |
| 195 | Abbi-gail | 200.00 |
| 196 | 14" | 125.00 |
| 196 | 19" | 125.00 |
| 196 | 10" Cowboy | 15.00 |
| 196 | 20" | 95.00 |
| 197 | 10" (N.O.) | 30.00 |
| 197 | Millie | 65.00 |
| 197 | 26" | 165.00 up |
| 198 | 9" | (no price available) |
| 198 | 14" (I.M.) | 25.00 |

# Schroeder's Antiques Price Guide

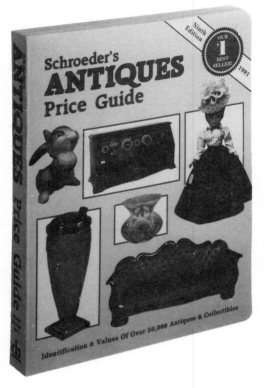

*Schroeder's Antiques Price Guide* has become THE household name in the antiques & collectibles industry. Our team of editors work year around with more than 200 contributors to bring you our #1 best-selling book on antiques & collectibles.

With more than 50,000 items identified & priced, *Schroeder's* is a must for the collector & dealer alike. If it merits the interest of today's collector, you'll find it in *Schroeder's.* Each subject is represented with histories and background information. In addition, hundreds of sharp original photos are used each year to illustrate not only the rare and unusual, but the everyday "fun-type" collectibles as well -- not postage stamp pictures, but large close-up shots that show important details clearly.

Our editors compile a new book each year. Never do we merely change prices. Accuracy is our primary aim. Prices are gathered over the entire year previous to publication, from ads and personal contacts. Then each category is thoroughly checked to spot inconsistencies, listings that may not be entirely reflective of actual market dealings, and lines too vague to be of merit. Only the best of the lot remains for publication. You'll find *Schroeder's Antiques Price Guide* the one to buy for factual information and quality.

No dealer, collector or investor can afford not to own this book. It is available from your favorite bookseller or antiques dealer at the low price of $12.95. If you are unable to find this price guide in your area, it's available from Collector Books, P.O. Box 3009, Paducah, KY 42002-3009 at $12.95 plus $2.00 for postage and handling.
**8½ x 11", 608 Pages**                                                     **$12.95**

**COLLECTOR BOOKS**
*A Division of Schroeder Publishing Co., Inc.*